Through Water & Ruin

For the people of Chesterfield.

Mushy Pea Publishing (UK)

Mushy Pea
Publishing

First published in 2024

Written by Joe Curtis
Designed by Megan Noble
Edited by Kim Kimber

ISBN: 978-1-0687785-1-3

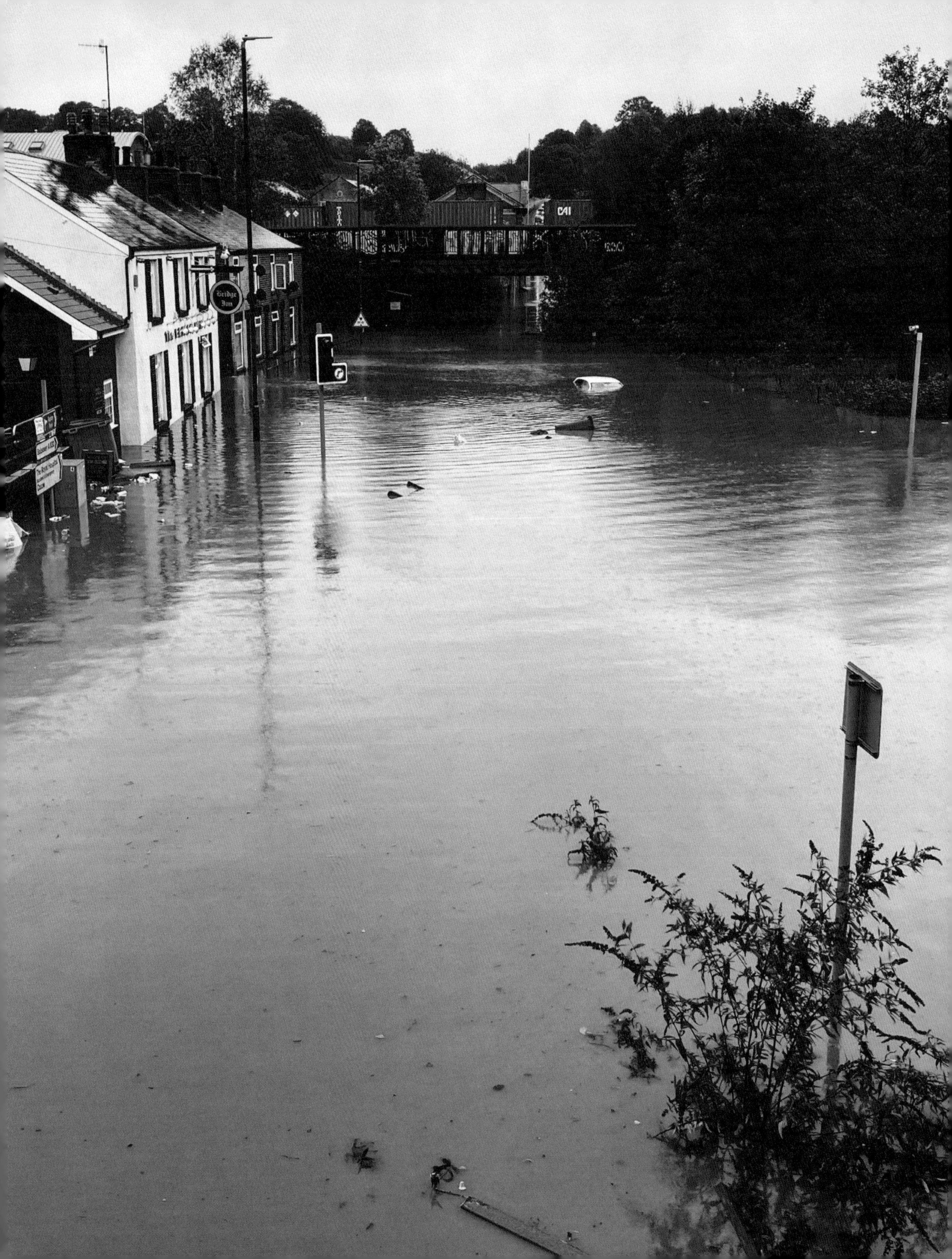

Bridge Inn
CAI

APOCALYPTIC!

It was the only way to describe the scene in front of us. It didn't feel real; a road I drive along every day was now a lake.

It had been raining all day without stopping. The same relentless drizzle that now broke the surface of the swirling, muddy water, ensuring we were all soaked.

I was with colleagues from work, John and Andrew, and we gazed dumbfounded at the flooded base of Hady Hill. We were not quite sure how to process the absurdity of the situation as yet another path was blocked. Where do we go from here? How would we get home? At the thought of 'home', I felt my stomach twist. An image of my cosy flat came to mind. Did I still have a home, or had it, too, been flooded?

It was the most surreal commute I've experienced. A race against time to negotiate the labyrinth of a flooded Chesterfield. And then deal with the consequences.

But let's start at the beginning...

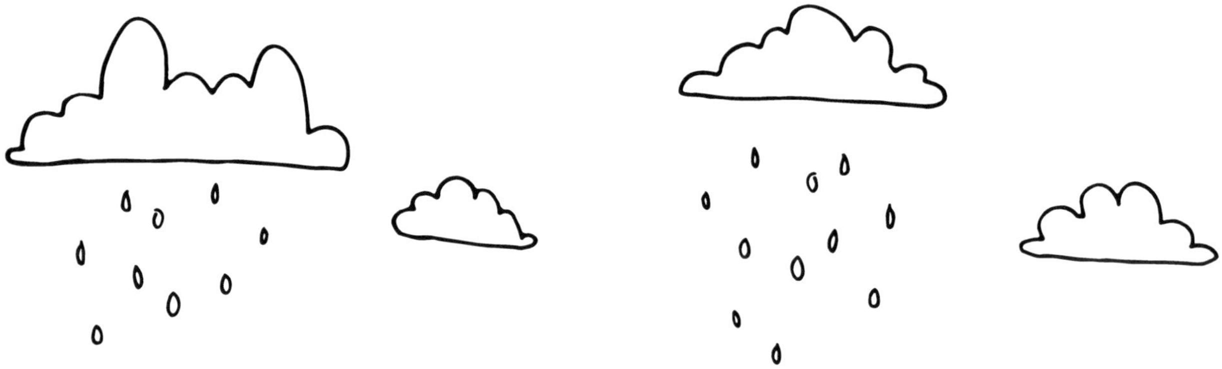

Chesterfield hosted a bleak Friday morning on 20 October 2023. It felt like any other autumn day. I was sitting in my living room sipping a coffee before work while reading a book. Looking to my right at the large windows of the old foundry building, I noticed the soft pitter-patter of rain, the sound filling an otherwise quiet room. Great, typical British weather!

Before long it was 8am, and I needed to set off for work. I sprung up and grabbed my bag. Looking back at my coffee table, I saw my empty mug and decided to tidy up later that evening. Locking my door behind me, I rushed straight down the corridor and through the main communal entrance.

As I turned left and headed down the path to my parking bay, I was greeted by a sheet of drizzle. My shoes audibly slapped the surface of water on the path as I walked. In hindsight this was strange as the path didn't usually accumulate that much water even when it was fully raining. However, my mind was on other things, and I was thinking about the projects I would be working on that day. As I fumbled with my car keys, ice-cold raindrops hit the back of my neck, making me grimace.

My windscreen wipers went on immediately, and the drizzle continued throughout my drive to work. It wasn't aggressive, but it was persistent. Unbroken grey cloud formed the entire sky, a sort of hopeless grey containing an endless supply of rain. I drove carefully through the thick coating of water on the roads. The traffic was worse than usual, but again, nothing struck me as being out of the ordinary.

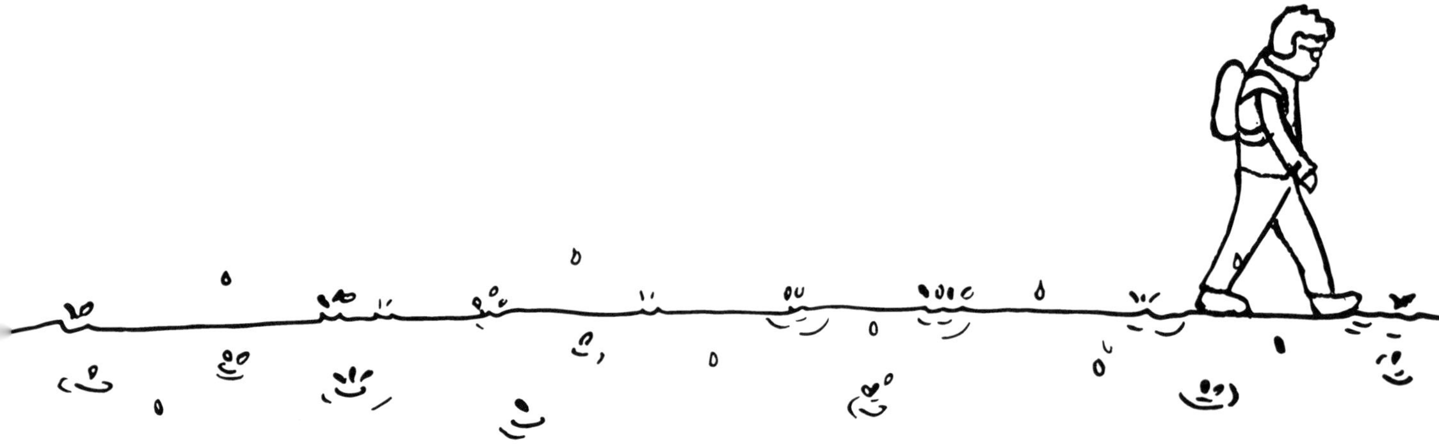

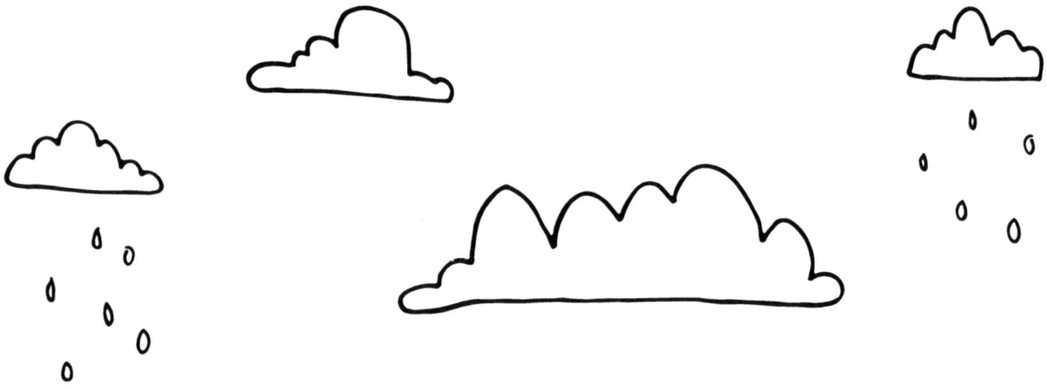

Pulling up at work, and alighting from my car, I once again had to face the drizzle. I reached inside for my bag and ran from the car park into the dry foyer. Relieved to have made it on time, I clocked in and began my morning routine.

Our factory employs about 100 people in total who, together, produce sustainable spiral wound paper containers. The packaging we make is used by well-known companies for such things as granulated gravy, coffee, milk substitutes, snacks, salt, cement and pet food, to name a few. Put it this way, you will either have previously owned a product that uses our packaging or have one on your shelf at this very moment.

My job is to help people remove frustrations and pain points from their day-to-day work. It's something I find incredibly satisfying. I work with everyone on site, across all departments. Everything from designing and prototyping components on production lines to developing and implementing IT systems. Most people would refer to this as being a continuous improvement coordinator.

I tend not to watch, read or listen to the news. So I was unaware there was a storm on the way. I did catch the odd conversation during the working day, but I must admit I didn't think anything was out of the ordinary, as everything tends to be exaggerated and dramatised in the media. I thought:

Oh, it's going to be a bit windy and wet. Nothing to worry about.

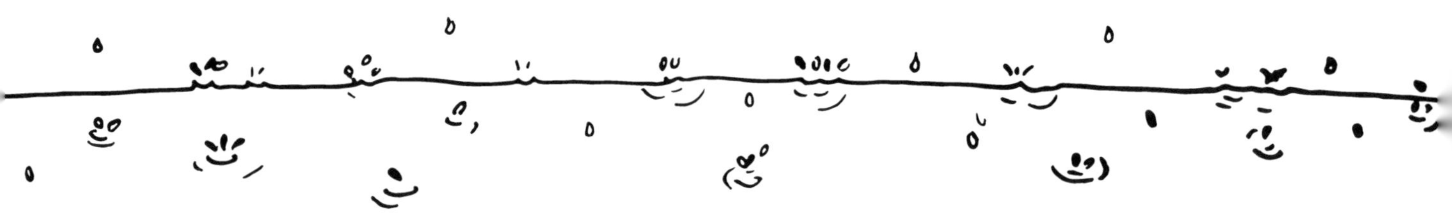

After attending the usual meetings and working on the factory floor until about 11am I returned to my desk. It was at this point we first began hearing about severe traffic jams due to surface water on the roads. This was a big problem as our company employs people who commute from Manchester, Derby and many other places. On hearing about the evolving situation, our manager, Andrew, made the decision to shut the plant so that people could get home.

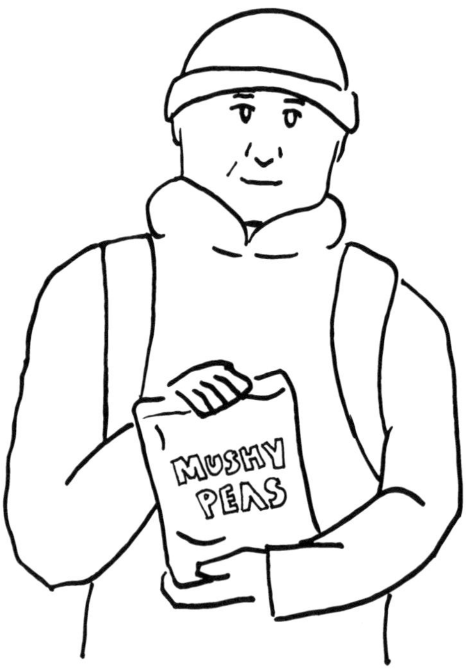

Andrew

I've known Andrew for about five years, and for the majority of that time he has been my boss. Andrew is middle-aged and into fitness. If he's not completed a gym workout or been for a run, he'll probably be planning to go out mountain biking later. He is very straight-talking and has a natural talent for seeing, and calling out, any nonsense (yes, I've replaced that last word to keep this PG). On this particular day, Andrew was wearing an orange jacket and carrying a green bag so you will easily be able to identify him in the photos.

Over the course of a few hours, production wound down and the plant was shut. An increasing list of road closures started to develop.

You'd hear someone shout out, 'They've just closed the road between the two big roundabouts near town,' followed by the inevitable, 'Oh no, I'll have to drive all the way around.'

Throughout the afternoon we received updates from our friends and colleagues about the progressively worsening situation, usually in the form of photos and videos. All shared the same narrative of standstill traffic and severe disruption to Chesterfield and its surrounding villages.

This wasn't looking good, was it?

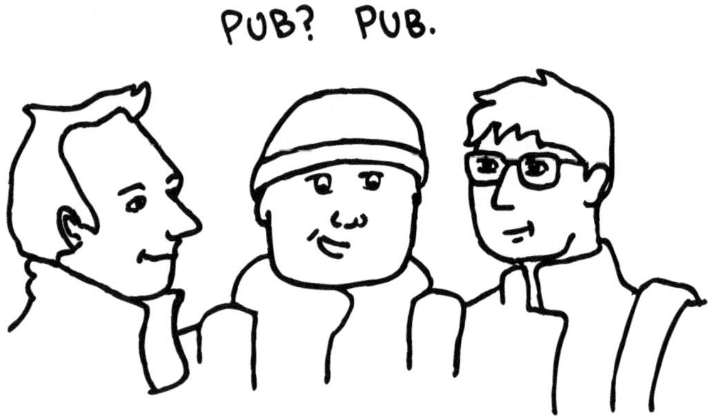

Trying to leave in a car was pointless due to the traffic issues. Andrew, John and I realised that we were all heading in the same direction to reach home, so we decided to walk as a group. It was during this time that we jovially agreed to stop off at a pub along the way and grab a pint together. We thought this would be a good way to break up the journey. At this point we had not grasped the full extent of the situation.

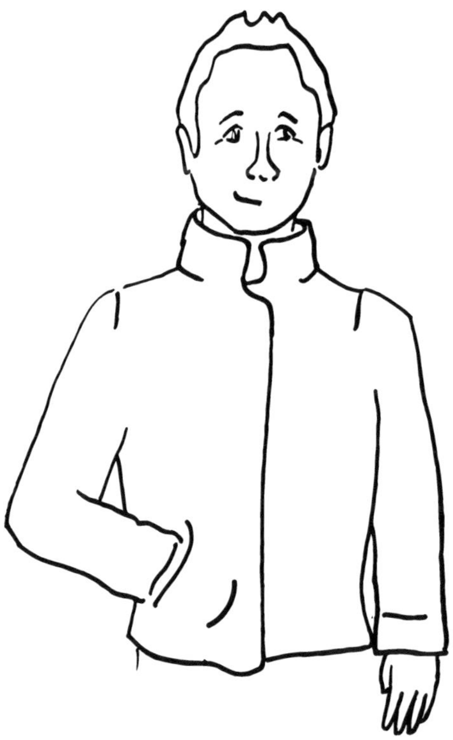

John

I've known John for around two years. He is also middle-aged. John oversees twelve people as the site's engineering manager. Our plant has ten production lines with a variety of machinery so keeping these maintained and working would be impossible without this team. Known for saying he's not competitive when in reality he is, John is a keen runner. You would know this if you spent five minutes in the open plan office with us. John can be identified in the photos as wearing a black jacket and black jeans.

By 1.50pm the plant had been fully shut down and we prepared to leave. I borrowed a thick, high-vis waterproof jacket from work and we secured our mobile phones in ziplock bags to prevent any water damage. This turned out to be a pointless exercise for me as I ended up with my phone in my hands more often than safely tucked away. Had this happened ten years ago, I'm certain my phone wouldn't have survived. Thankfully, the waterproofing of these devices has really improved, along with the functionality.

When I walked outside, I faced the same drizzle I had met in the morning. Bizarrely, it never seemed to change, no matter how many hours passed; the rain continued to fall at the exact same rate. Luckily, I had a pair of wellies in the back of my car and thought it would be a good idea to change into them.

I decided to take my work rucksack with me, with my normal shoes stored safely in a bag in the back. This was to keep them dry in case I needed to change shoes later on. I also took an umbrella with me.

We noticed that traffic heading in all directions was at a standstill on the usually empty road outside of our factory. This is something neither I, nor any of my work colleagues, had seen before. Just as we were about to set off, Andrew said:

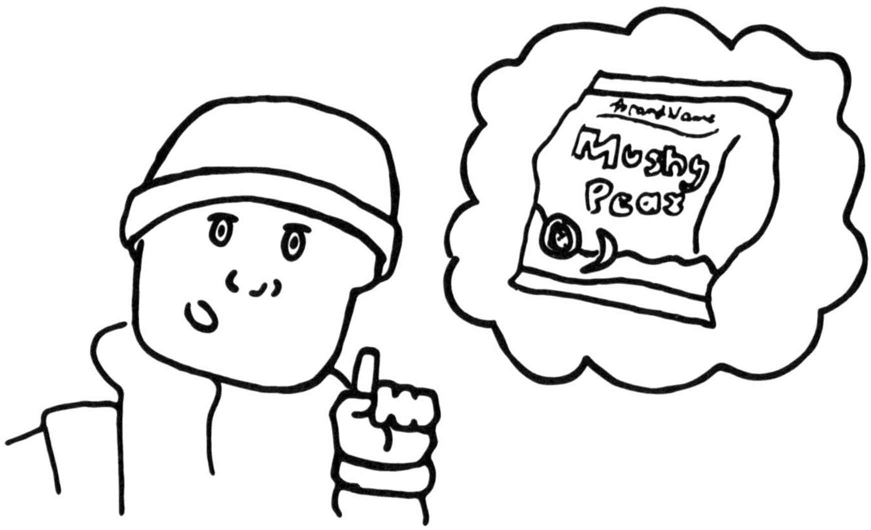

'MY PEAS!' before returning inside to retrieve a bag of frozen mushy peas from the freezer, which he placed in his rucksack.

I was heading for Camlough Walk, Andrew for Calow and John for Shirebrook. Basically, we all needed to head east, which was simple enough in theory. Thanks to the intel provided by our colleagues, we already knew that Dock Walk was a no go. Instead, we tried to circle around it by taking Boythorpe Avenue intending to rejoin Boythorpe Road slightly higher up.

It was at that junction we first saw flooding for ourselves, although the police had cordoned off the road, meaning I could only take photos from a distance. Andrew chuckled slightly and said:

'Well, we couldn't have gone Dock Walk way.'

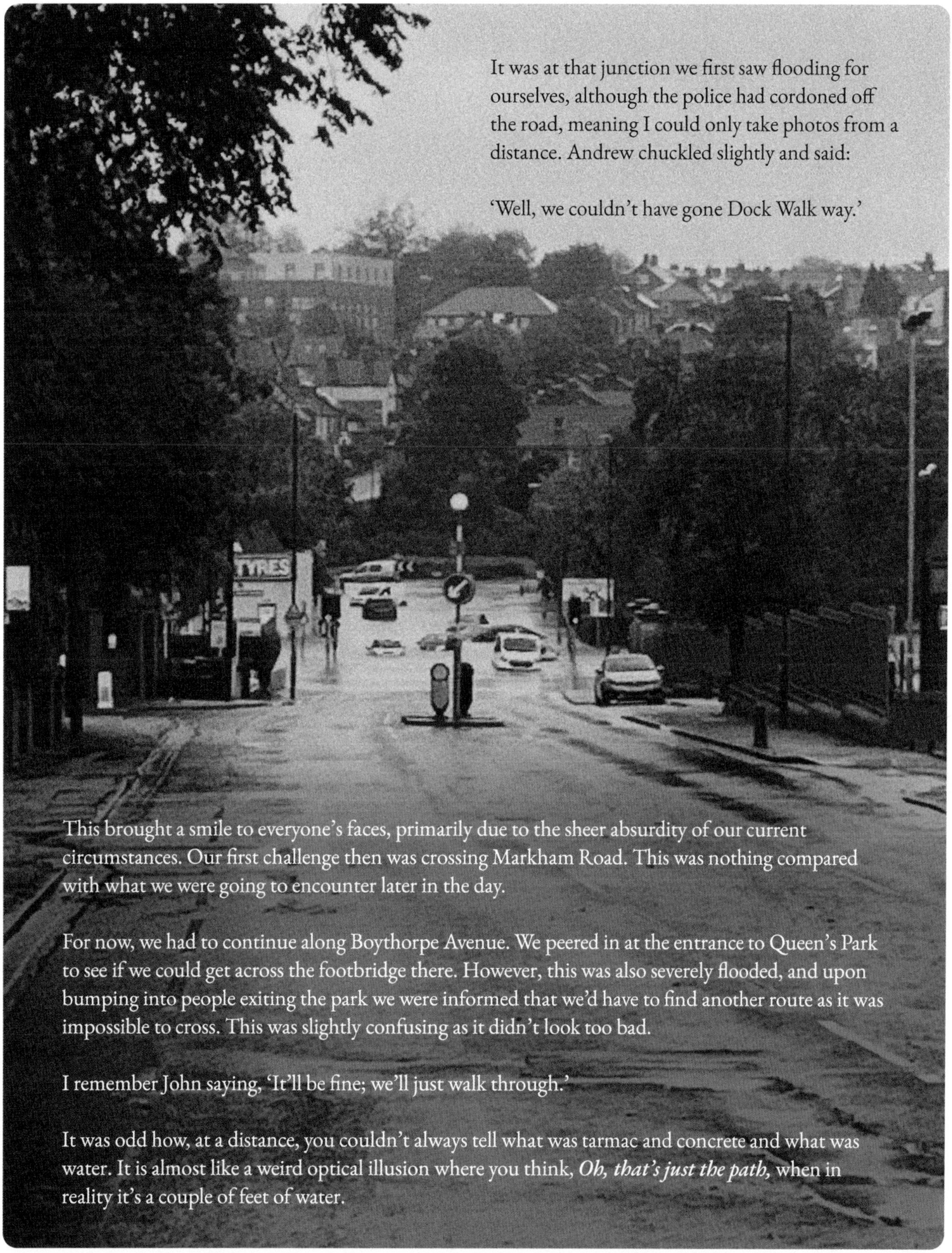

This brought a smile to everyone's faces, primarily due to the sheer absurdity of our current circumstances. Our first challenge then was crossing Markham Road. This was nothing compared with what we were going to encounter later in the day.

For now, we had to continue along Boythorpe Avenue. We peered in at the entrance to Queen's Park to see if we could get across the footbridge there. However, this was also severely flooded, and upon bumping into people exiting the park we were informed that we'd have to find another route as it was impossible to cross. This was slightly confusing as it didn't look too bad.

I remember John saying, 'It'll be fine; we'll just walk through.'

It was odd how, at a distance, you couldn't always tell what was tarmac and concrete and what was water. It is almost like a weird optical illusion where you think, *Oh, that's just the path,* when in reality it's a couple of feet of water.

We stepped forward a few paces and Andrew said:

'Ah, no, John, look at that lamppost, you can see the waterline on it. It's high that. Come on, we can go around.' John paused for a moment, contemplating.

'I think we can walk through it,' he said. I shook my head, and the three of us stood still, unsure whether or not to go forward or back.

'Okay,' said John eventually. 'It's probably safer to go another way.' I sighed, feeling relieved, as we retraced our steps. Unfortunately, I didn't take any photos here, but with only the camera on my phone, I don't think you'd have seen much at that distance.

The next junction we made it to was Park Road. Looking left, we could see Markham Road was flooded, too. With no police cordon to stop us, we decided to walk down and see the chaos up close.

The River Hipper runs right under this junction (from left to right in the photos). Coincidently, there is a measurement station located at this very junction, with the information available on the government website. On this day it was about two and a half metres higher than the top of its nominal range. That's the average ceiling height of most homes in the UK. The River Hipper is a tributary of the River Rother; the latter flows directly past my flat.

It was strange seeing the traffic lights still operating even though there was a good couple of feet of water. Some cars attempted to drive through it, with water crashing over their bonnets and engines choking as a result. I wonder how many of these cars died the next day due to being forced to wade through this water.

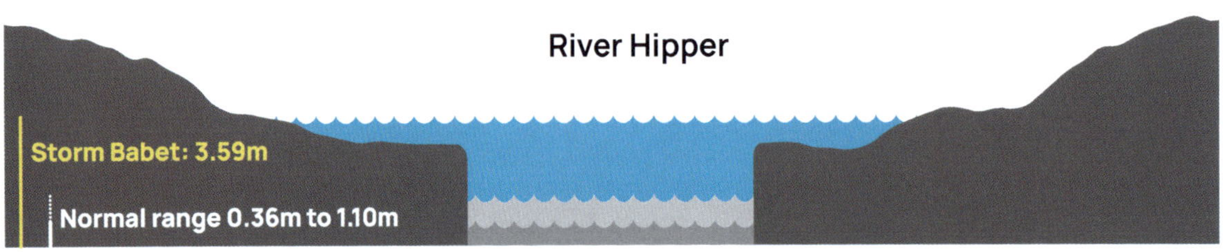

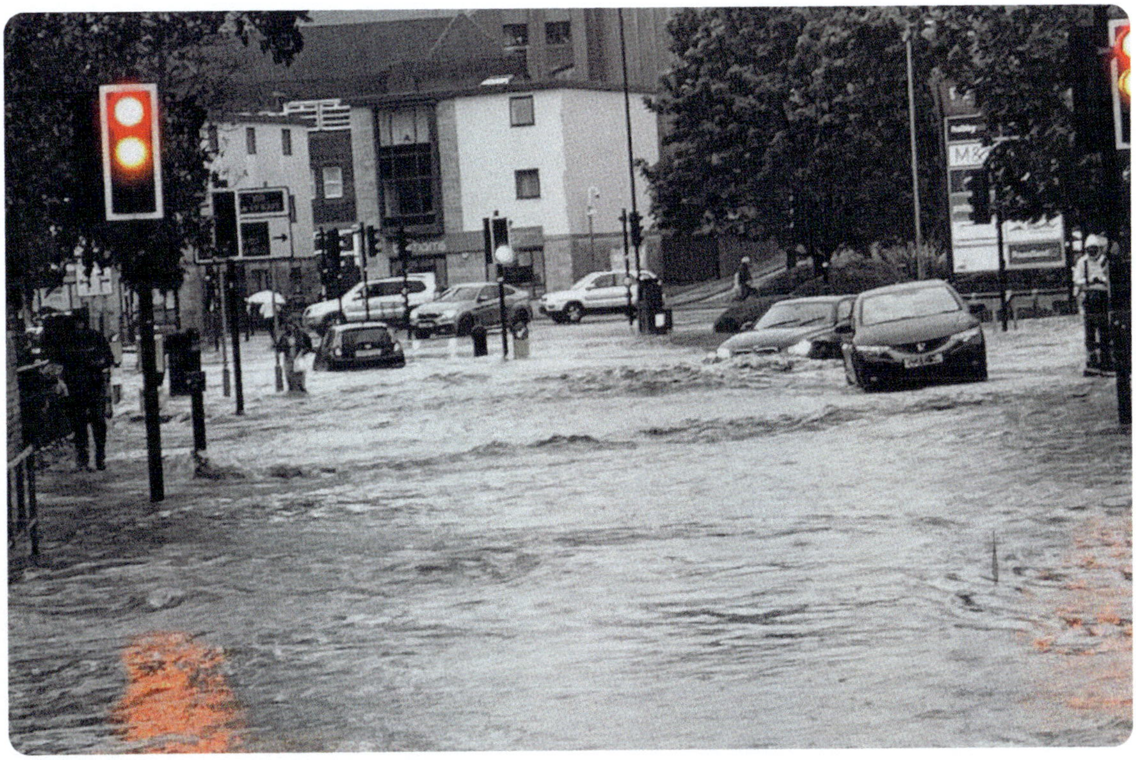

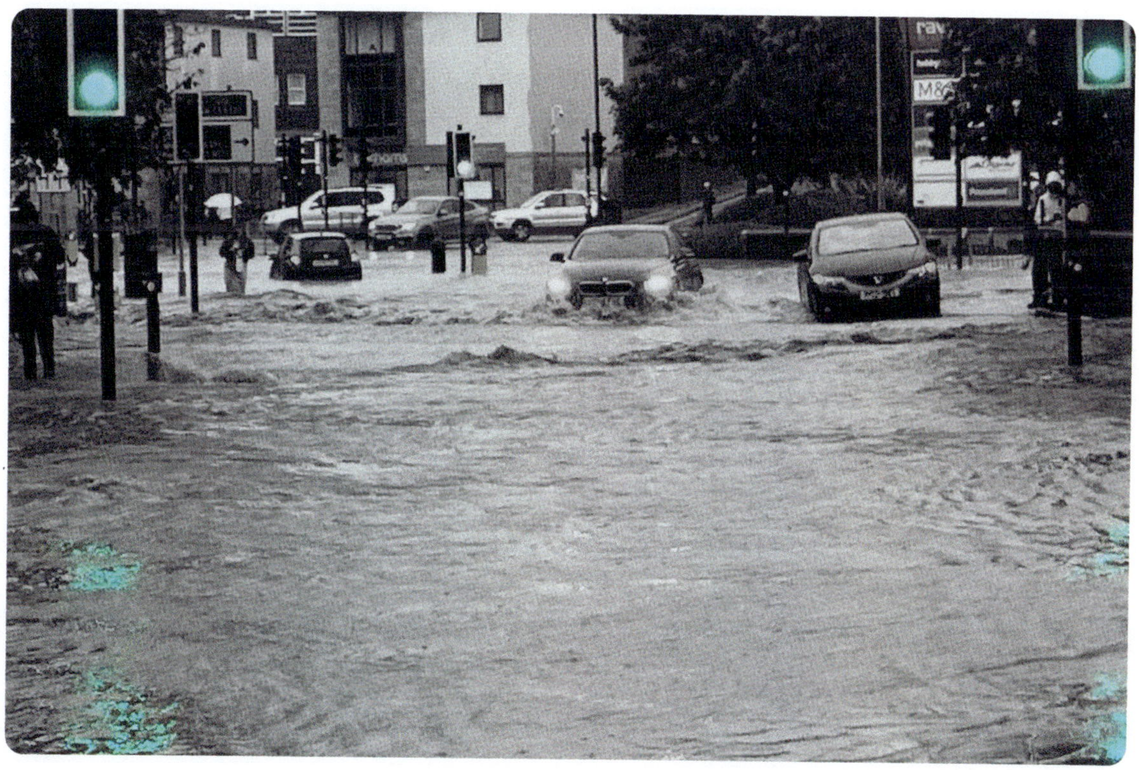

Half a dozen people stood around in disbelief. Water lapped at the terrace houses lining Park Road, and I hoped the level wouldn't rise further. Every second that passed seemed to increase the tension for those people who were seemingly on the edge of having water break into their homes. I pondered if this would be the fate of my flat.

The A619, aka Markham Road, was the road I commuted into work on every day. Today it became a divide, cutting Chesterfield in half between the south and north. With no other option, we walked along Baden Powell Road. Andrew had remembered a snicket he thought would be a good cut-through and would allow us to cross Markham Road at the high point near Lordsmill Roundabout.

Andrew was originally from Burnley, having moved to Chesterfield about ten years ago. I have no idea how he knew about this obscure cut-through, which doesn't shout for attention. He also was quick to point out that in Burnley this is called a 'ginnel', but I didn't think this was a real word! Turns out it is though, a ginnel being defined as a narrow passage or alley between buildings. John calls this a 'jitty' and I would call it a 'tenfoot'. Interesting how we all have specific colloquialisms for describing the most random things. Don't get me started on the breadcake – cob argument!

Sure enough, just past the local off-licence, we found it. Again, I didn't take many photos on this part of our journey. At one point you can see Spire Walk Retail Park, the gym there clearly flooded.

'Well, it looks like I won't be going to the gym on Monday,' said Andrew.

John and I laughed at the thought of Andrew doing a workout with water up to his knees.

Following the path further, it took us over the River Hipper, which was very full, and ended up at the top of Ravenside Retail Park. From here you could see the flooded car park and shops, many of which didn't open for months afterwards.

The route had popped us out onto Markham Road and, sure enough, the higher elevation meant this section remained unflooded. We were easily able to cross over and get into Chesterfield town centre. We would have had a far greater challenge in getting home had we not been able to cross at this point.

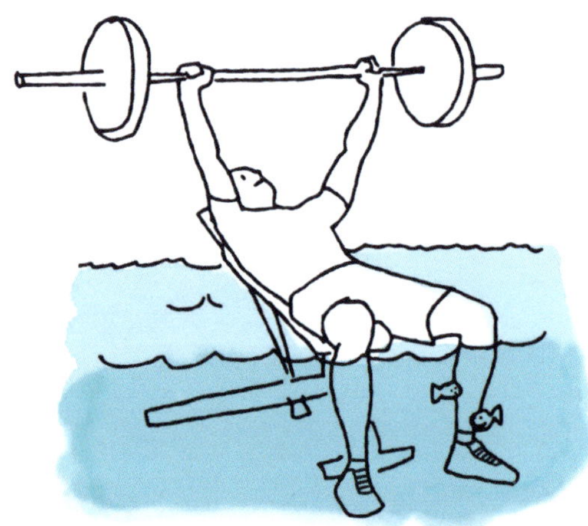

It kept raining for the entire journey, and we were all soaked as it had been about an hour and twenty minutes since we left work. As per our original plan, we decided to stop for a couple of pints in the Pig and Pump pub, which involved a short detour up the hill into Chesterfield town centre. I ordered a beer called 'White Rat', but a more apt name at

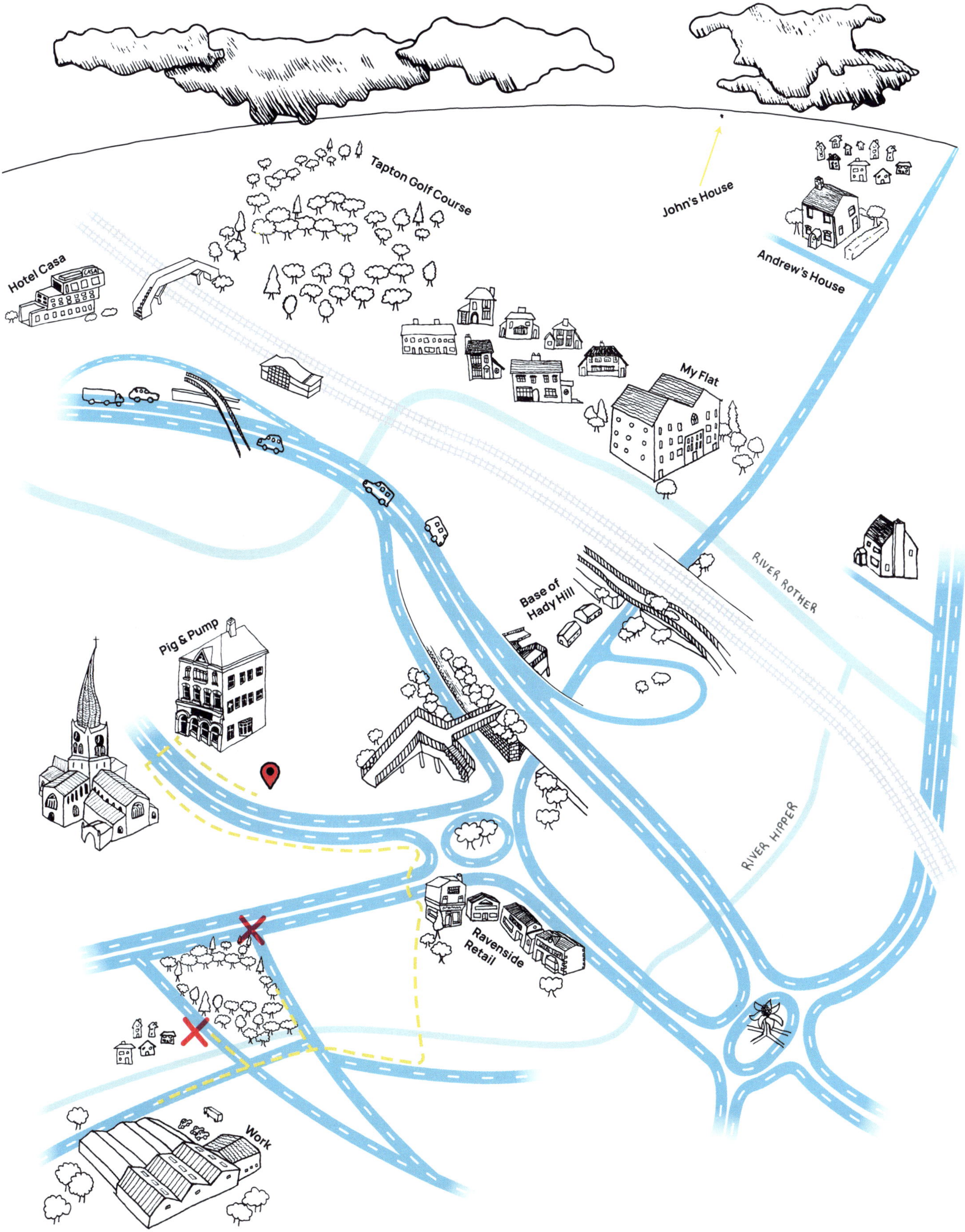
Tapton Golf Course
John's House
Hotel Casa
Andrew's House
My Flat
River Rother
Base of Hady Hill
Pig & Pump
River Hipper
Ravenside Retail
Work

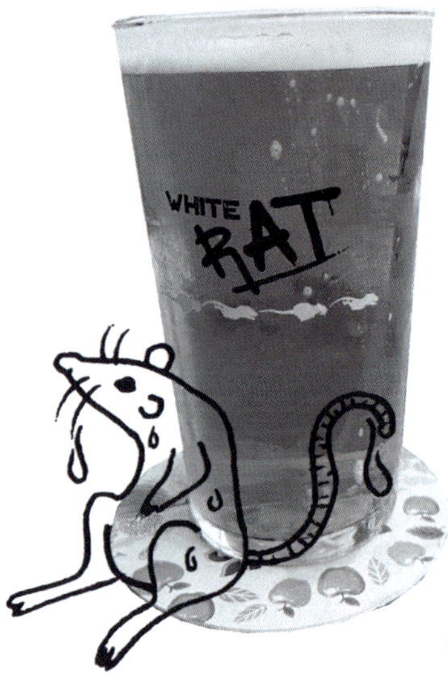

that time would've been 'Drowned Rat'. That's certainly how I felt anyway! If nothing else, it was a good opportunity to dry out slightly and have a break.

During our time there we struck up a conversation with a lovely elderly lady who lived in one of the surrounding villages and was waiting to be picked up because she was stranded in the town centre. We shared the best information we had based on our experiences and wished her luck in getting home that evening.

You'll be relieved to know that Andrew's mushy peas still seemed to be okay. In fact, he made a point of checking them and informing us of their status. I'm not sure why, but we were starting to get quite invested in the peas making it back safely.

Three pints later, we left the pub and headed over the pedestrian bridge that tunnels under Rother Way and leads to Hady Hill (A632). It's only now, as I write this, that I realise how bizarre this sounds; it's an elevated bridge tunnel over and then through a road. Absolute nonsense, right? Well, put it like this: Initially you walk over a bridge before entering the tunnel; the bridge goes over a slip road for Rother Way. That's still not clear? Maybe a photo or illustration will help to explain it better.

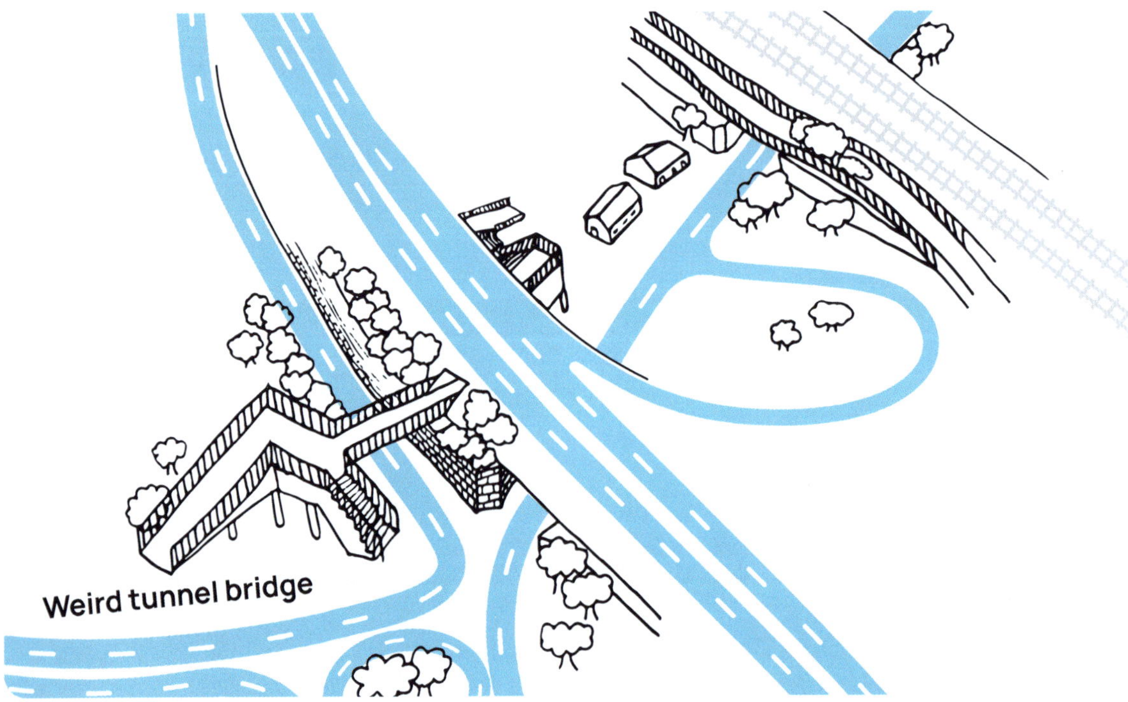

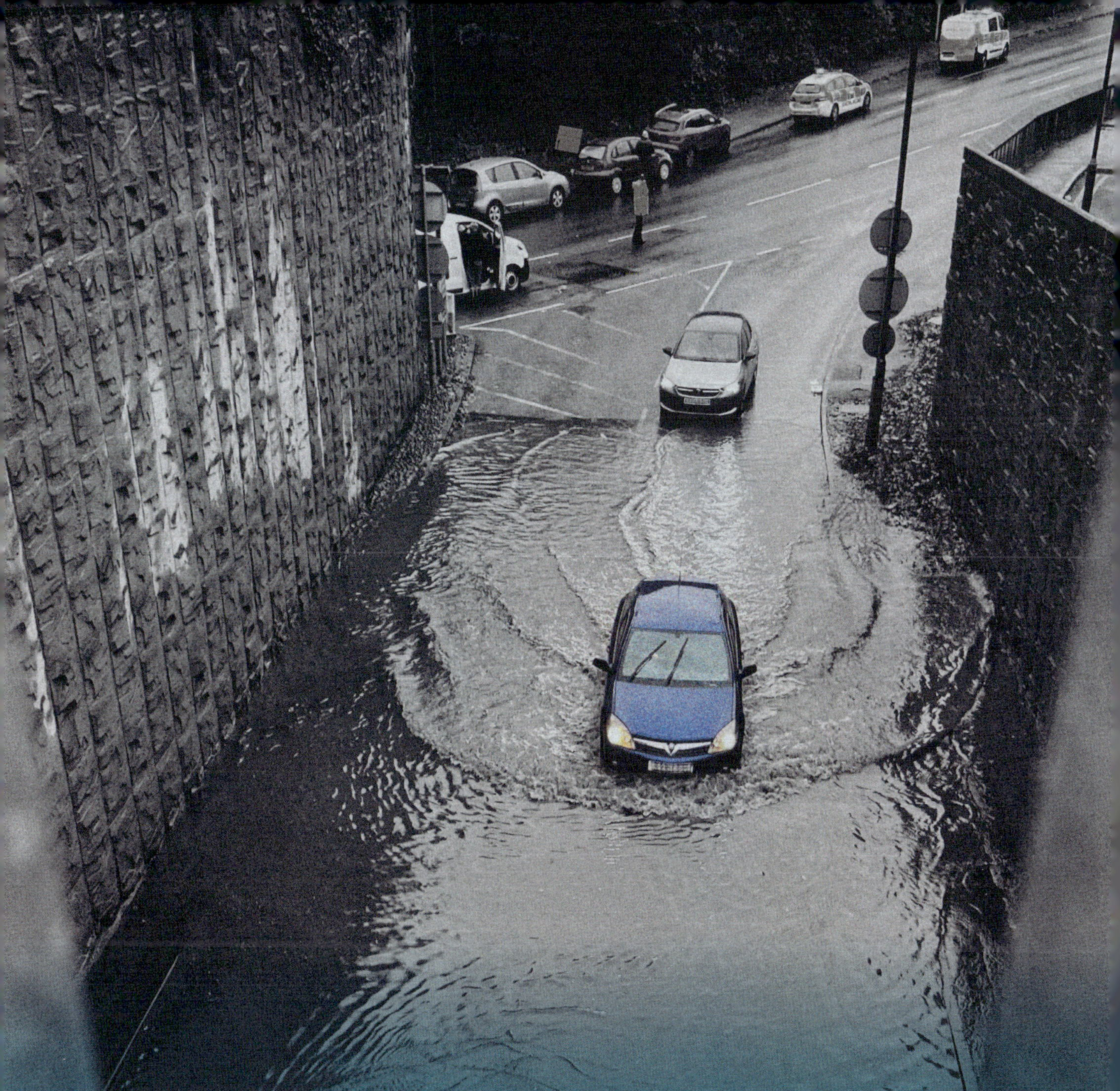

I noticed that there was a fair build-up of water at the bottom of the slip road and that the police had blocked off Hady Hill to traffic before the tunnel. This wasn't a good sign. The tunnel takes you under Rother Way and spits you out at the base of Hady Hill.

Nothing could have prepared me for the sight at the end of that tunnel. It looked like a lake, not a main road into Chesterfield. One of the first things to strike me was a car with only the roof visible above the waterline. What you can't see is the car under the bridge, because it's completely submerged, only to be revealed once the water had drained away. At the time we had no clue it was there.

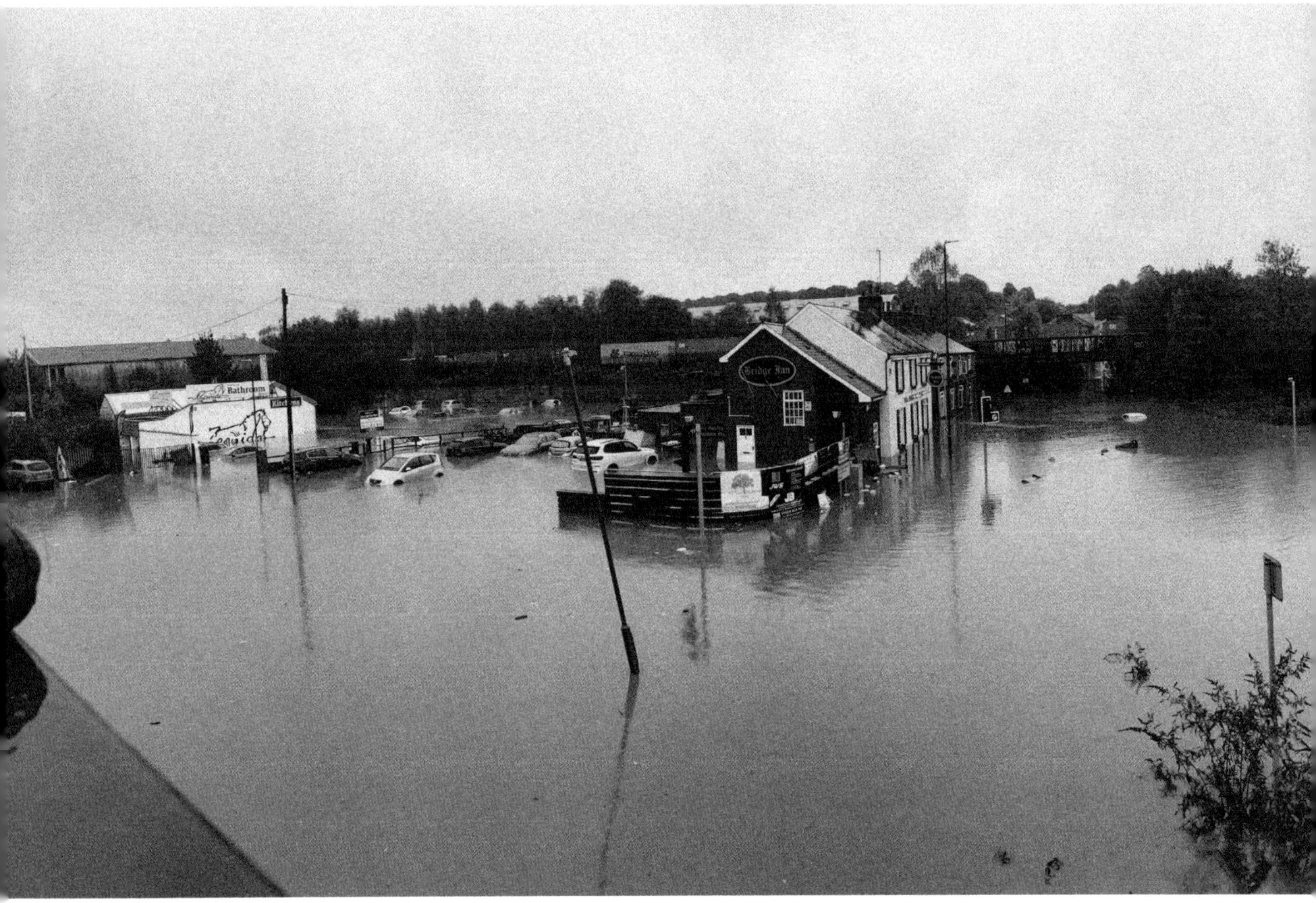
Bathroom
Bridge Inn

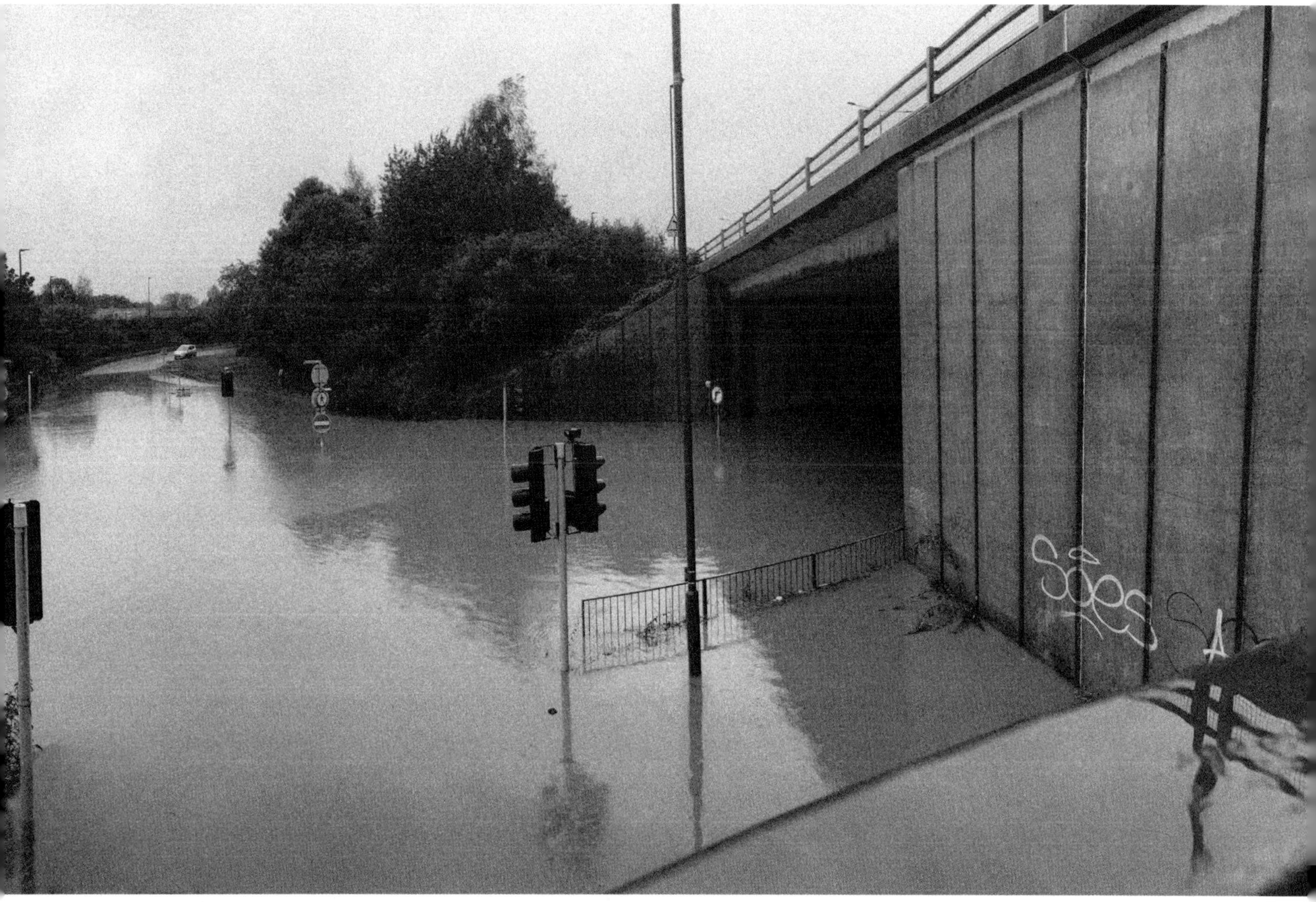

The entire scene in front of me was more like an apocalypse film than reality. Andrew's reaction was a solitary, 'Wow!' I was speechless. We all stood there for a moment, silently trying to process the situation.

The water was completely opaque; murky brown with assorted detritus and people's possessions floating in it. The same sky hung over everything like a blanket of grey doom. The same drizzle added to the expanse of water blocking our path. The familiar problem of 'How do we get over there?' returned. Yet again we had to figure out how to cross this expanse of water.

I may only be twenty-six, but I have experienced two flood events in my life. The terrible 2007 floods, while living in Hull as a child, and now this. I vividly remember having to move classrooms at primary school before our parents came to collect us. I saw the devastation first-hand then, too, but that pales in comparison to what I saw before me.

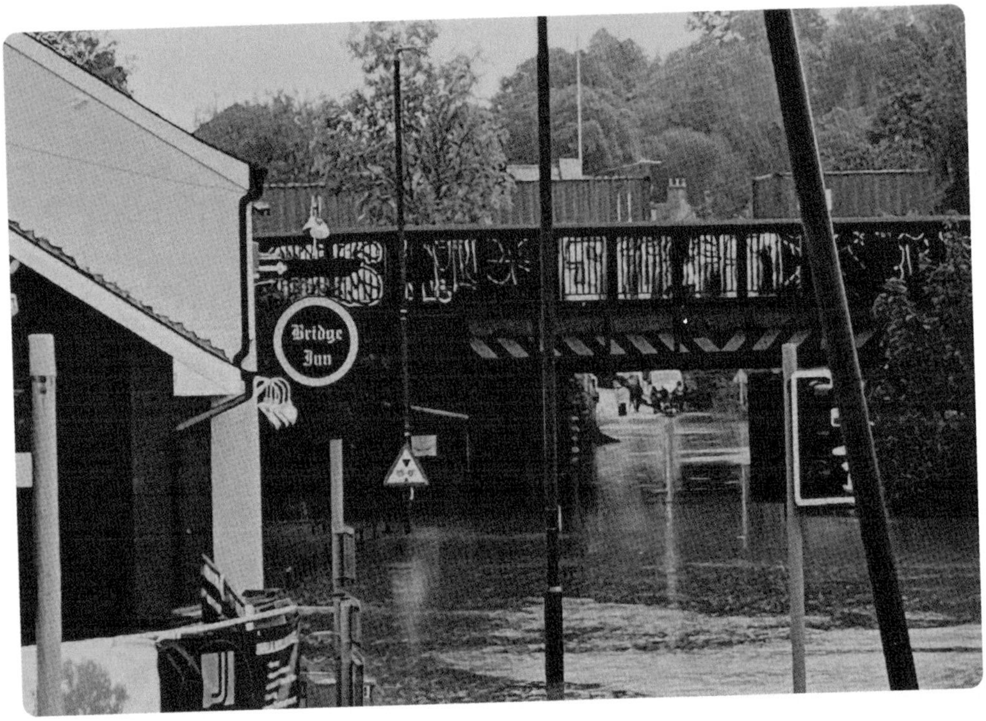
Bridge
Inn

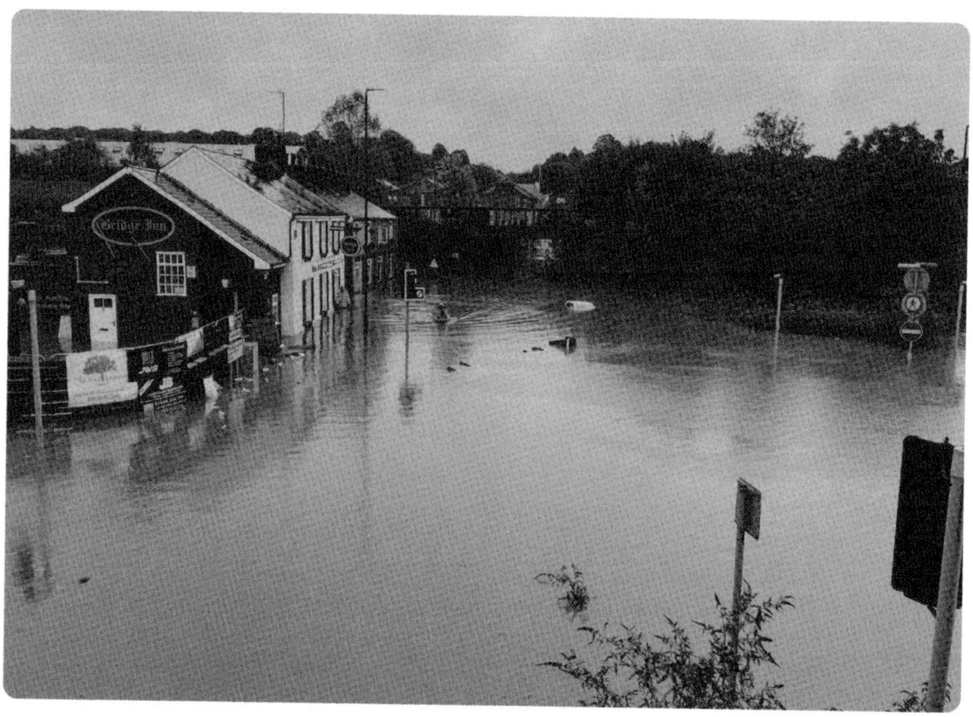
Bridge Inn

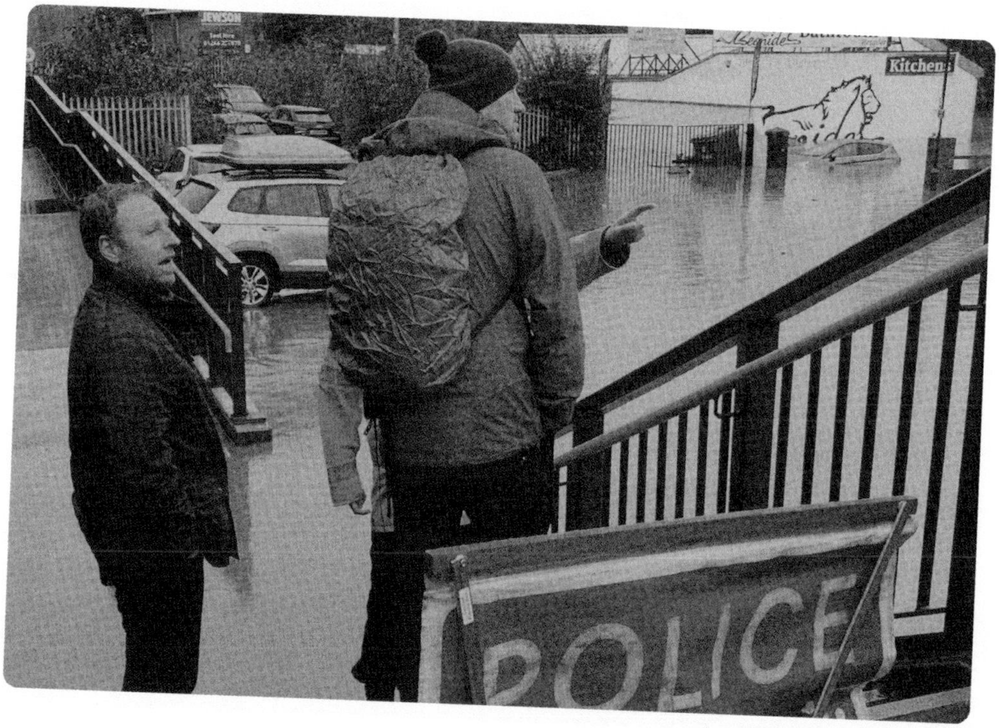
JEWSON
Kitchens
POLICE

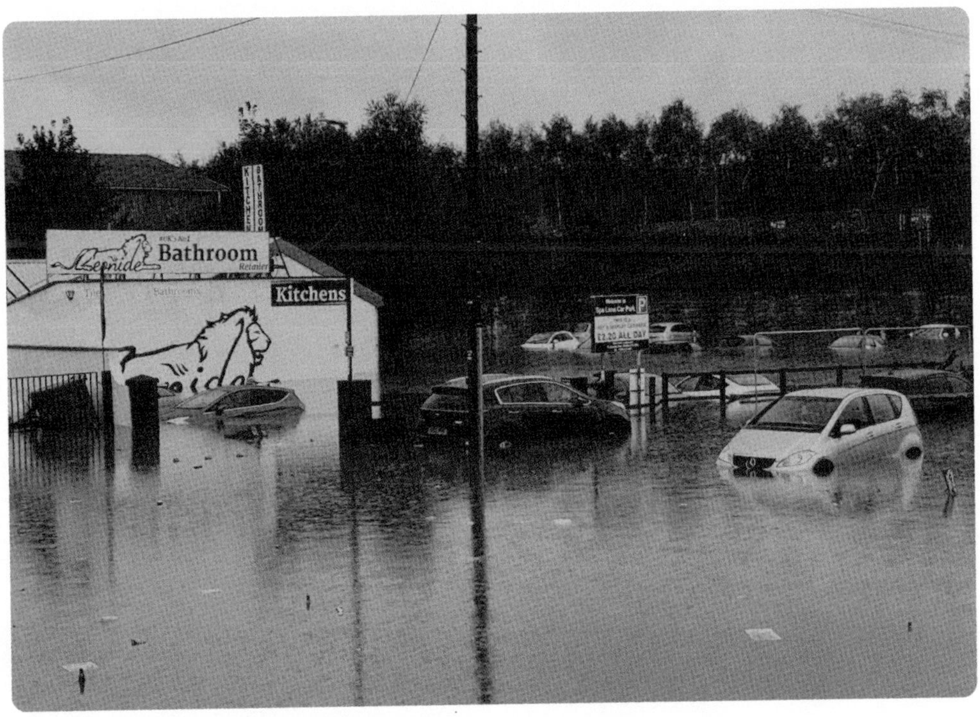
Bathroom
Kitchens
£3.20 ALL DAY

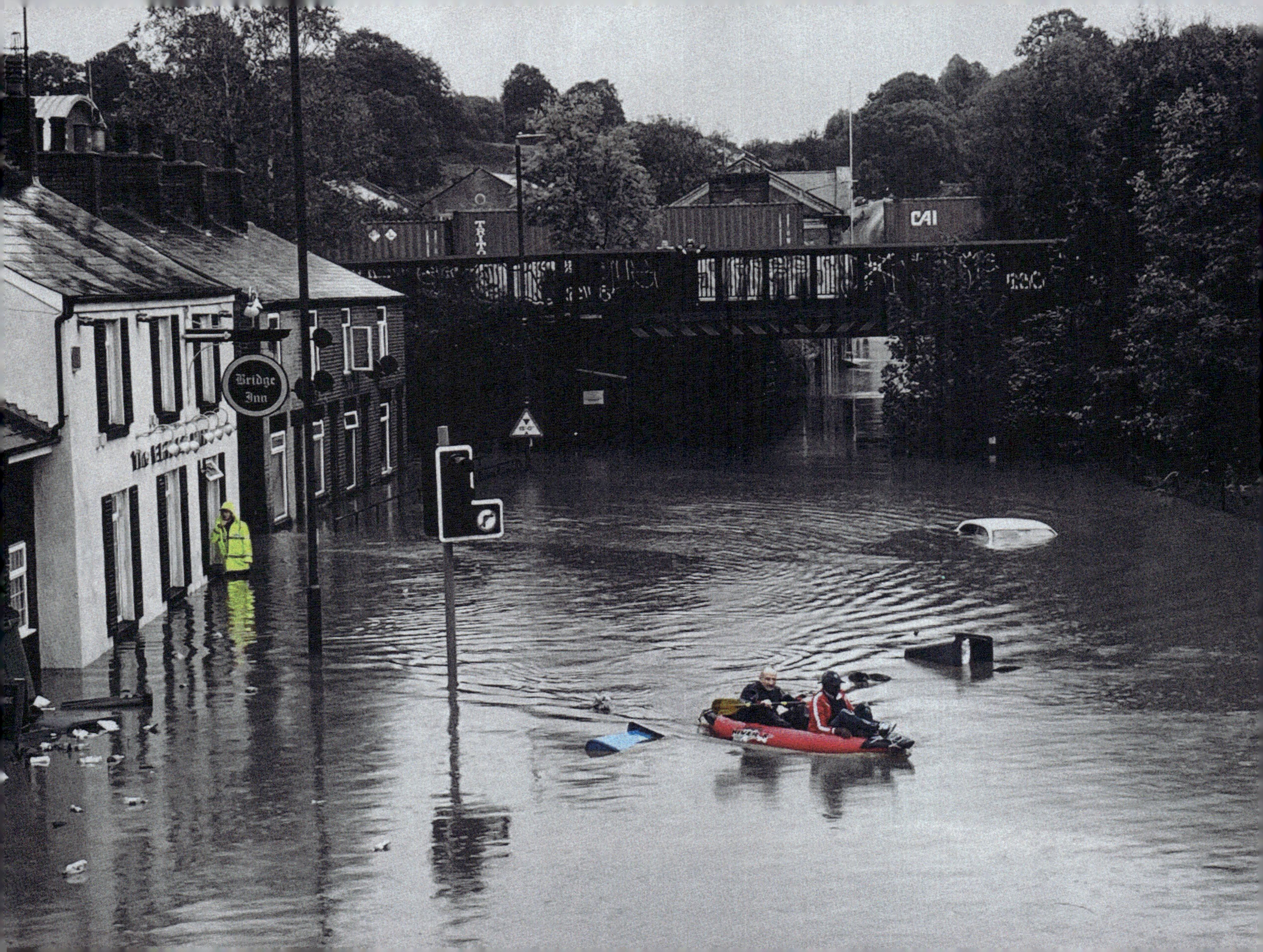
Bridge Inn
CAI

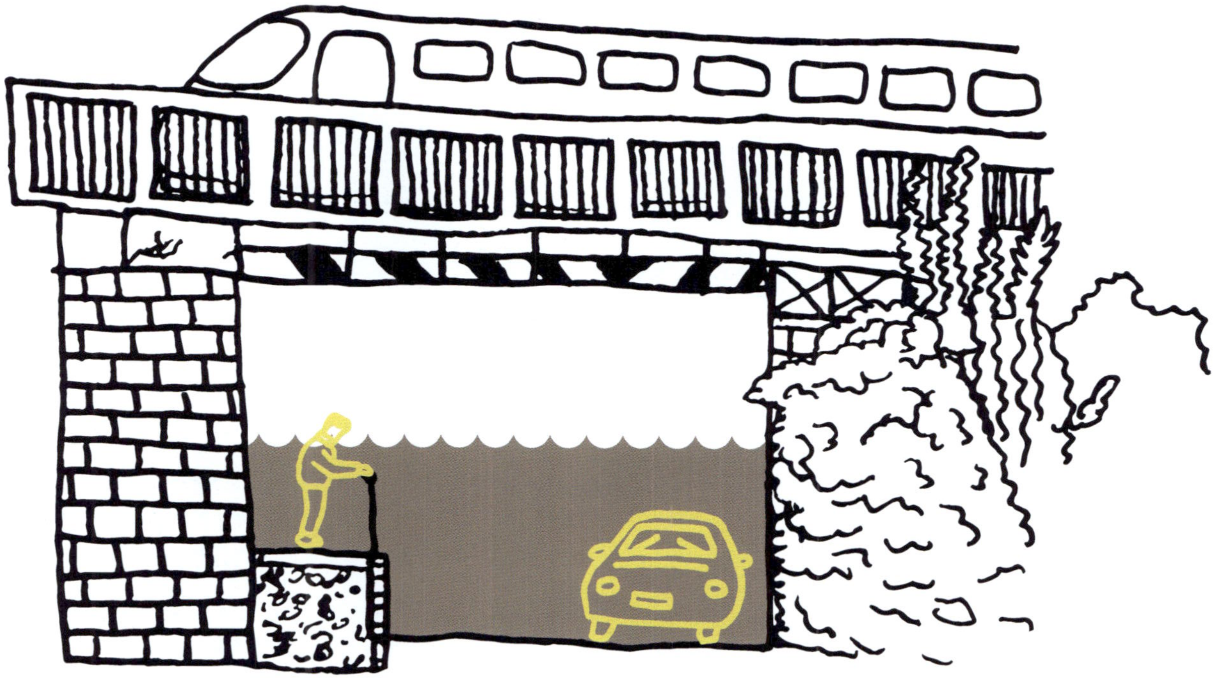

Base of Hady Hill where the water was approximately 2m deep.

Vehicles parked in Spa Lane Car Park flashed their hazards and lights, thinking they were perhaps being robbed. There must have been at least twenty completely flooded out cars in this area alone. Strangely, one or two were floating and bobbing about slightly, while some were clearly fixed in position. I wondered why some vehicles were behaving differently to others? And, if given enough time, would they all sink and fix themselves to the road once again?

A row of terraced houses and the Bridge Inn were also completely flooded on the ground floor. I felt sorry for the people who lived there and hoped they all had somewhere to stay that night. Hopefully, they were all insured too.

Again, there was a police block to stop people from going further. Stationed there was someone who became known to us as Officer Tiddlywink. This is obviously not his real name, but the one I shall be using.

One of the strangest sights was a man paddling up and down this main road on a kayak. I believe he was rescuing people from flooded houses, as Andrew did ask if we could get a lift across from this man but was told no. If the situation had not been so serious, it would have been amusing watching him navigate around the floating bins and debris. His passengers sat on the front of the kayak, clinging on so as not to fall into the lake.

Officer Tiddlywink didn't have any advice on how to reach our destination.

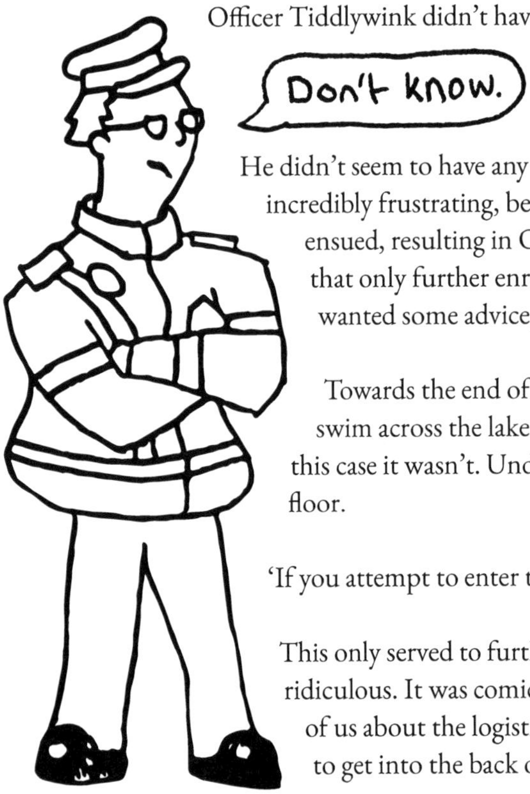

he said, offering no help beyond this.

He didn't seem to have any interest in assisting us. John found the officer's attitude incredibly frustrating, becoming more irate as time went on. A heated discussion ensued, resulting in Officer Tiddlywink turning on his body camera, a move that only further enraged John. To be fair, John was frustrated as he only wanted some advice, though being fuelled with beer probably didn't help.

Towards the end of the discussion, John threatened to get in the water and swim across the lake. The depth of flood water is often exaggerated, but in this case it wasn't. Under the bridge, it would have been too deep to touch the floor.

'If you attempt to enter the water you'll get done for it,' said Tiddlywink.

This only served to further antagonise our companion who thought this was ridiculous. It was comical how much discussion followed between the three of us about the logistics of how this would work and that John would have to get into the back of a police car soaking wet. At one point, Andrew even joked that he might still get home quicker, which made me laugh. I had visions of John jumping in and swimming across only to see him arrested on the other side and then returned via Kayak Man.

As the rambling debate between John and Tiddlywink continued, I was busy taking photos. With John distracting 'Mr Useful', I could wander about and shoot hassle-free. I even managed to walk down the stairs a short distance so that I was able to see under the bridge to the other side of the road. From this angle you could see a more substantial police road block with multiple cars and more police. I glanced at John and Tiddlywink, their conversation carrying over to where I was standing.

'Look, we just want to get home,' John said reasonably. 'I'm asking which way to go. You're supposed to serve citizens in need, and I'm a citizen in need!'

'I don't know,' Tiddywink replied, emphasising each word, 'but you'll have to find another way.'

'I can see that. But which way? Surely you must know which routes are blocked!'

Tiddlywink shrugged.

I then noticed Andrew staring at his phone deep in concentration, looking at maps. I took this as my cue to join him to help find an alternative way around.

The situation was other-worldly. I don't think I've ever experienced such a bizarre scenario. While John continued the 'ahem' debate he was having with PC Tiddlywink, Andrew calmly asked, 'Is it okay round the back of the train station?'

'I said that I don't know.'

'Could you radio through and ask if we can get around that way?' said Andrew.

A reasonable request; however, this was met with a scowl and a firm 'no'. I could hear John chuntering in the background about how ridiculous this was.

In total, we spent just under a quarter of an hour there, before agreeing to try and go around the back of Chesterfield train station with a view to pick up Crow Lane and circle around the lake that had formed at the base of Hady Hill. After convincing John not to swim across and tearing him away from his new best friend, we set off towards the train station.

Upon exiting the weird bridge tunnel, we turned right onto Mill Street, following it up to the footbridge at Corporation Street. During this part of our journey, we chatted with a couple of people trying to figure out how to navigate this newly-formed divide across Chesterfield, just as we were.

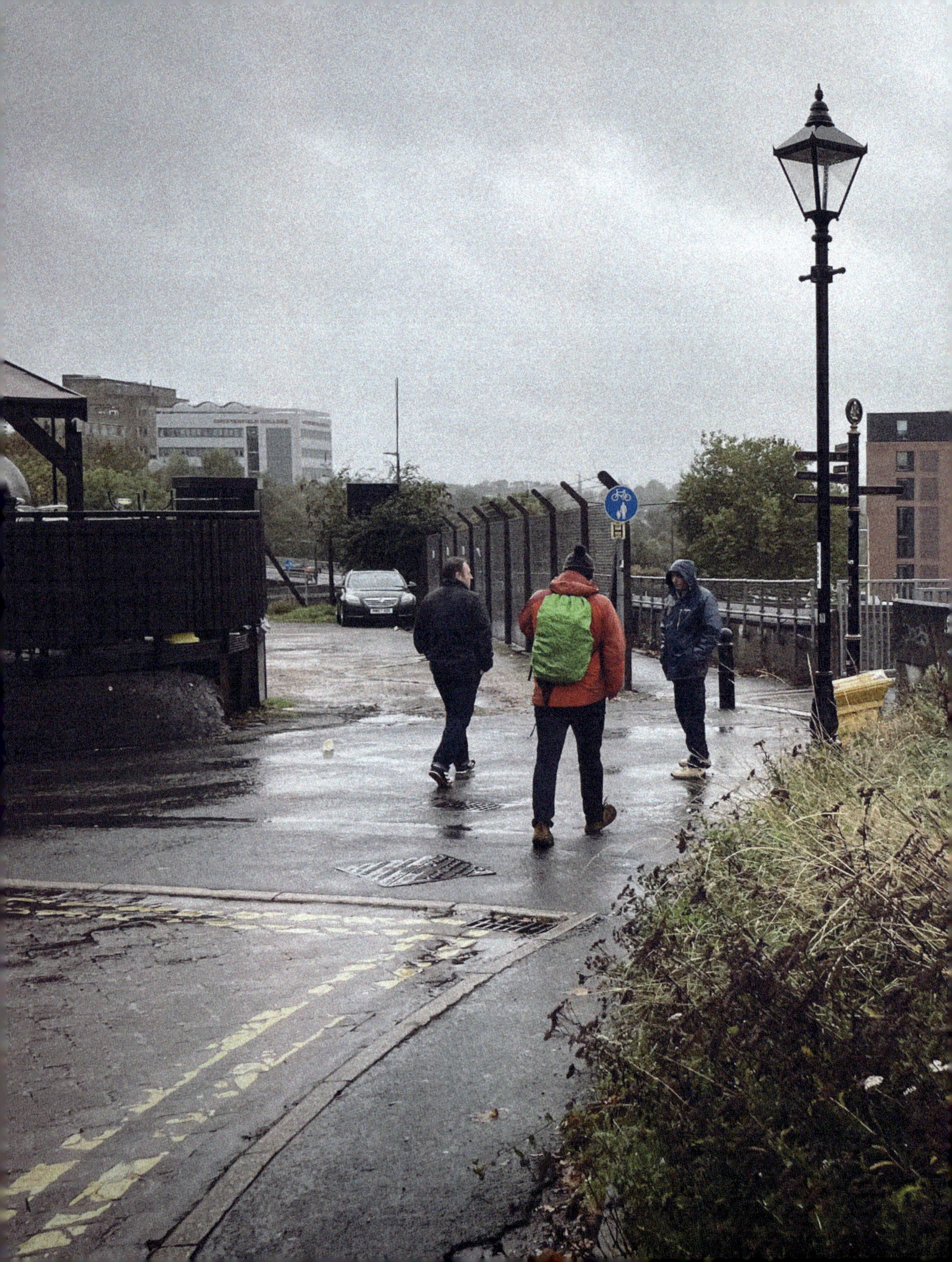

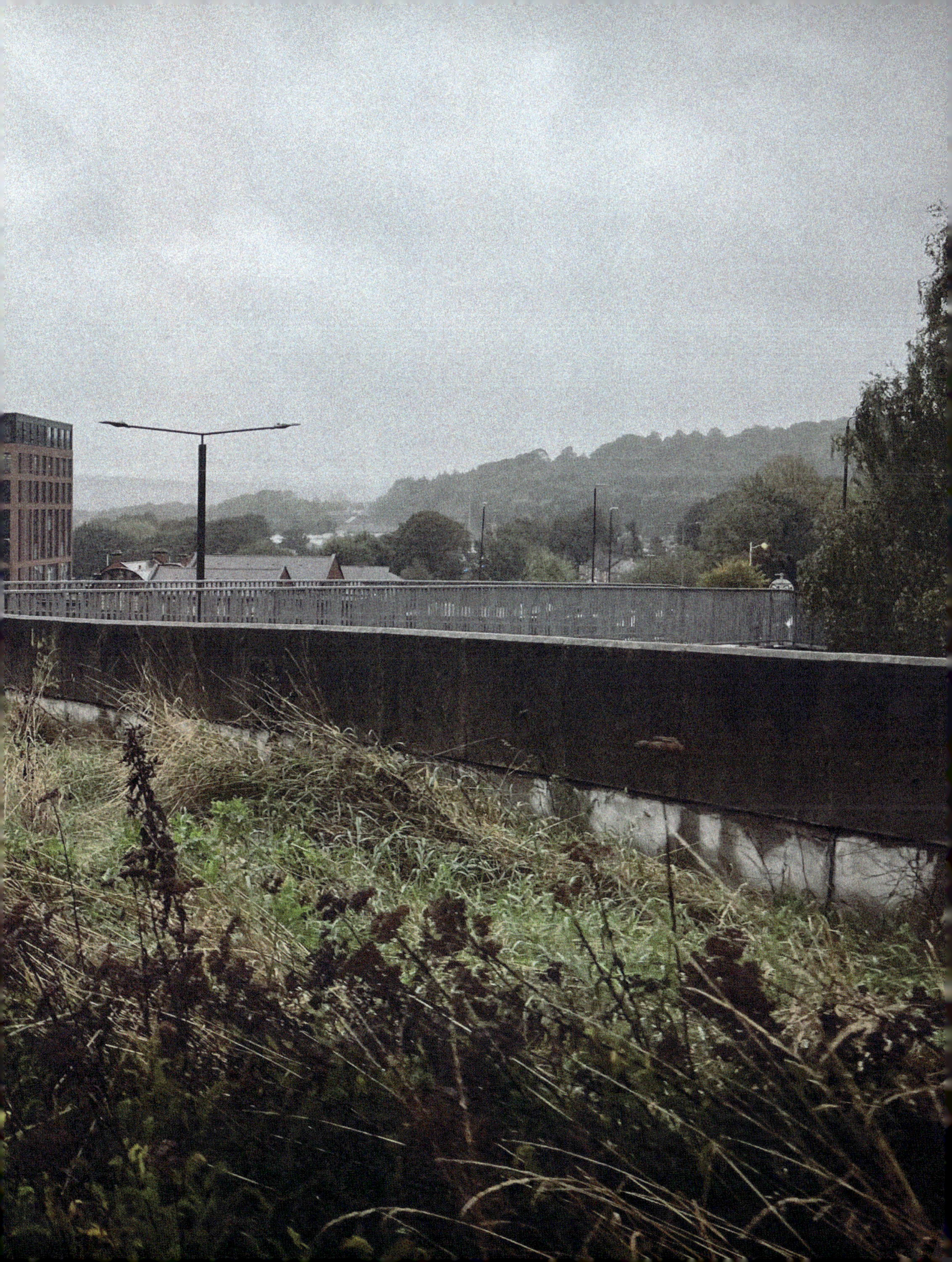

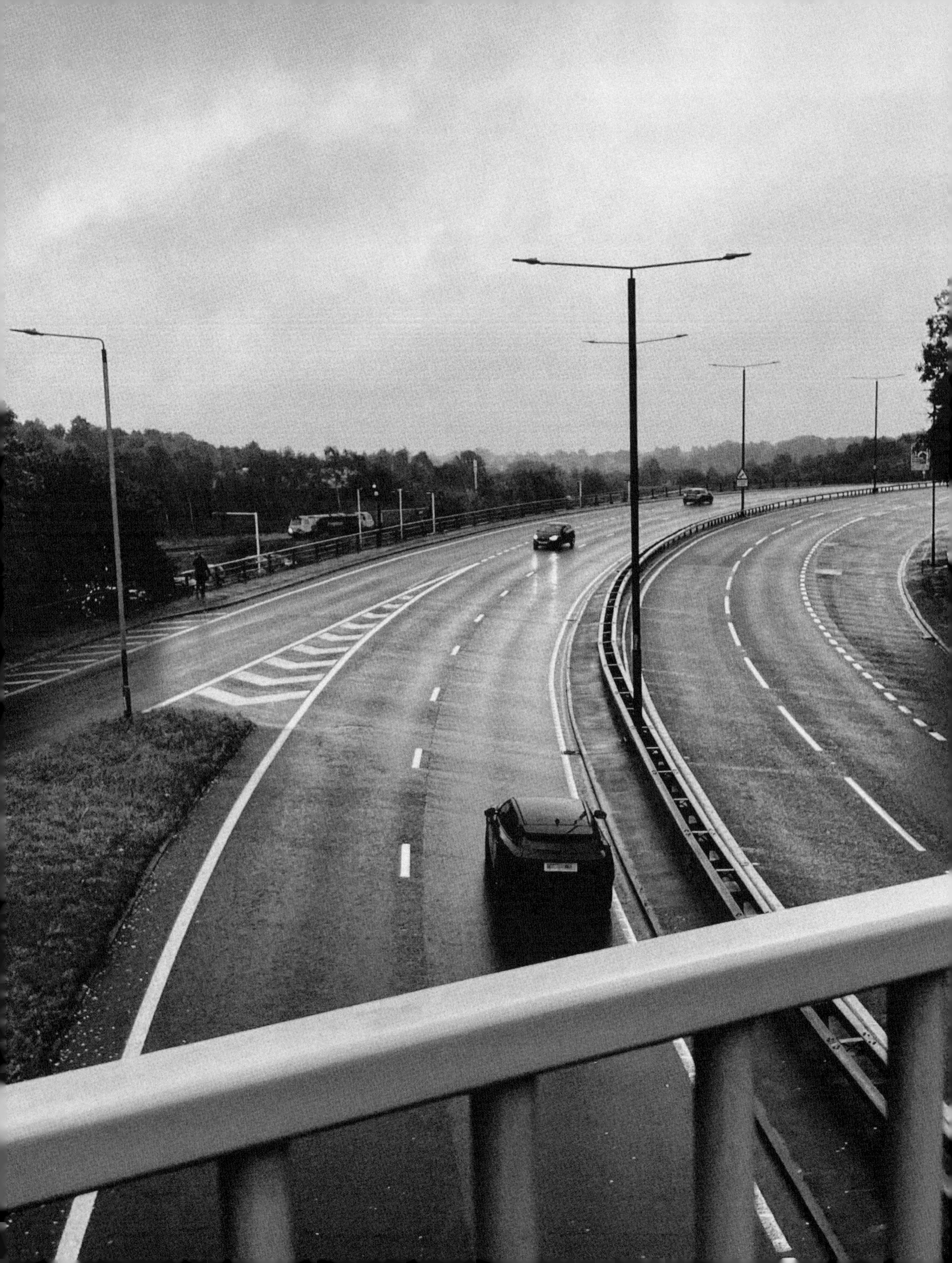

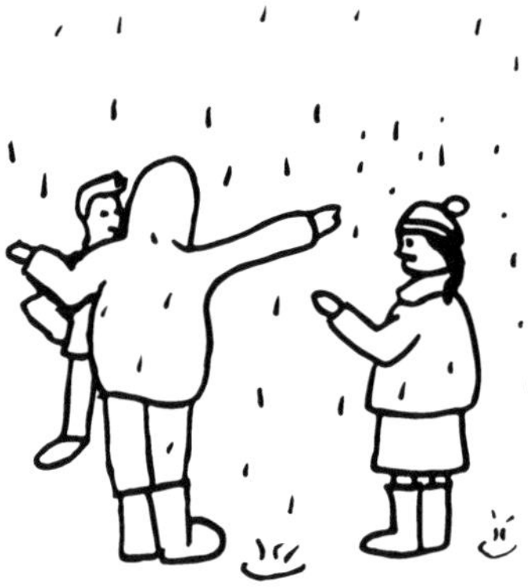

Everyone's experiences were the same though, having to re-route numerous times in order to try and find a way around. It united us and, in a weird sort of way, you could feel the camaraderie between them when people talked. Complete strangers, yet here we were exchanging information and working as a team.

While on the footbridge I noticed something amiss out of the corner of my eye; a car was travelling the wrong way down the left lane of Rother Way. It was an odd sight and clearly demonstrated the sheer desperation people felt to find a way home. I wonder what thoughts were going through that driver's mind for them to consider driving the wrong way down a dual carriageway. I guess this was their equivalent of 'swimming' through the lake.

After crossing the bridge, we saw the train station and turned right onto Crow Lane. Large shrubs and trees block the view as you walk round the sweeping bend on the approach to the railway bridge. You could hear the unmistakable sound of rushing water as we drew closer. The kind of sound you get with rapids in a voluminous river. As we rounded the corner, we saw gushing torrents of water going through the fence on the left hand side, with an incredibly full River Rother.

Another familiar sight greeted us, a car drowned with just its roof exposed. So far, every flooded roadway we had encountered had at least one sunk vehicle. I'm not talking about parked vehicles here, but rather ones in the middle of a lane. Clearly, the owner had tried to get through a partially flooded road, and the car had stalled and then become stuck.

John, still slightly irate from his encounter with Tiddlywink, wanted to 'swim' across again. I genuinely thought he was going to attempt it. His frustration and body language, at one point, looked like he was going to go for it. I'm sure you'll see what I mean in the photo with John looking towards the railway bridge.

Through the tunnel (see picture, page 33) you can see a couple of people on the other side of Crow Lane. I expect they were in a parallel situation to us, trying to figure out which way around they could take. I wondered if they, too, had come from Hady Hill and if we would cross them at a later point in our journey.

Thankfully, Andrew and I managed to convince John to try and find another way around. The railings on the left hand side of the photo show how much water was coursing through the gaps. I'm sure this would have been enough to sweep you away, and this is what we pointed out to John to help convince him to find a different way with us.

Bear in mind that one metre cubed of water, or about the volume of ten standard baths, weighs around 1000kg. If that starts flowing, or pushing you into something, you aren't going to stand much of a chance. This also raises an interesting point; at some places the water would have easily exceeded a metre deep.

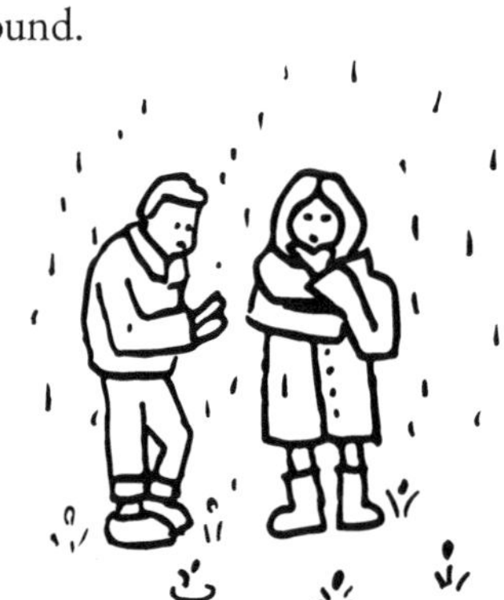

This fact was hammered home on 28 December 2023. Five storms after Babet the country hosted Gerrit. A storm that brought damaging winds and heavy rain to the UK, further contributing to an already wet few months.

Suffice to say, Gerrit caused its own carnage, too much for me to go into within this book. I will mention that there was severe travel disruption to the rail network and roads. Huge crowds were stuck at King's Cross railway station, motorists were stranded on the A9 and the M48 Severn Bridge was shut.

In North Yorkshire the River Esk runs from Westerdale to Whitby where it meets the North Sea. Along that path it passes through two small villages called Lealholm & Glaisdale. Lealholm is connected to Glaisdale via Rake Lane, a single track road that is popular with 4x4 enthusiasts due to the ford that crosses the River Esk.

My friend Scott was very much into off-roading in 4x4 vehicles. This usually involved driving on challenging 'green lanes', potentially getting stuck then having to get unstuck. I'd known him for roughly ten years at this point with him being a year older than myself.

On the day in question, he was a passenger in a two-tonne 4x4 vehicle with two other men. They were in a small convoy with other enthusiasts and the first to approach the ford at around 11.45am that morning.

Mid-crossing, their vehicle was swept into the river and dragged 400 yards downstream. It came to rest fully submerged beneath the surface of the water. Scott didn't make it across the River Esk that day; he never made it out of the car. No one did.

One of my close friends rang me the day after to break the news. I still remember the utter bewilderment upon hearing it. The confusion, the questions. At the time there wasn't a lot of information available. We were all simply shocked and devastated.

I thought back to Christmas Eve, when I was out at the pub with a couple of friends. I remember one of them ringing Scott and trying to get him to come out and meet us. Unfortunately, he couldn't join us. I had hoped we would see him on New Year's Eve, sadly that never happened.

First-hand accounts, taken from the inquest reports in October 2024, stated that the River Esk was about 1.2m deep according to the level marker boards. The closest official level meter is at Lealholm, slightly upstream of the crossing point. Although Storm Gerrit had contributed to the water level, it was still within its nominal range (of up to 1.8m according to the government website). That's not to say the level wasn't high, it was. I just wanted to point out that even when at a 'nominal' level rivers are incredibly powerful forces.

The events experienced by those men and their respective families are awful. It is not my intention to tell their story. Nor do I have any right to. I had been writing this book when I got told the news, which made me think of all the flooded cars I saw. All the flooded houses I saw. All the flooded crossings I saw. Each of these areas had the potential to claim life, and at least one did.

On the 25 January 2024, I attended Scott's funeral. I listened to the eulogies, I thought about how quickly things can go wrong, and how a single decision can change your life. Or end it.

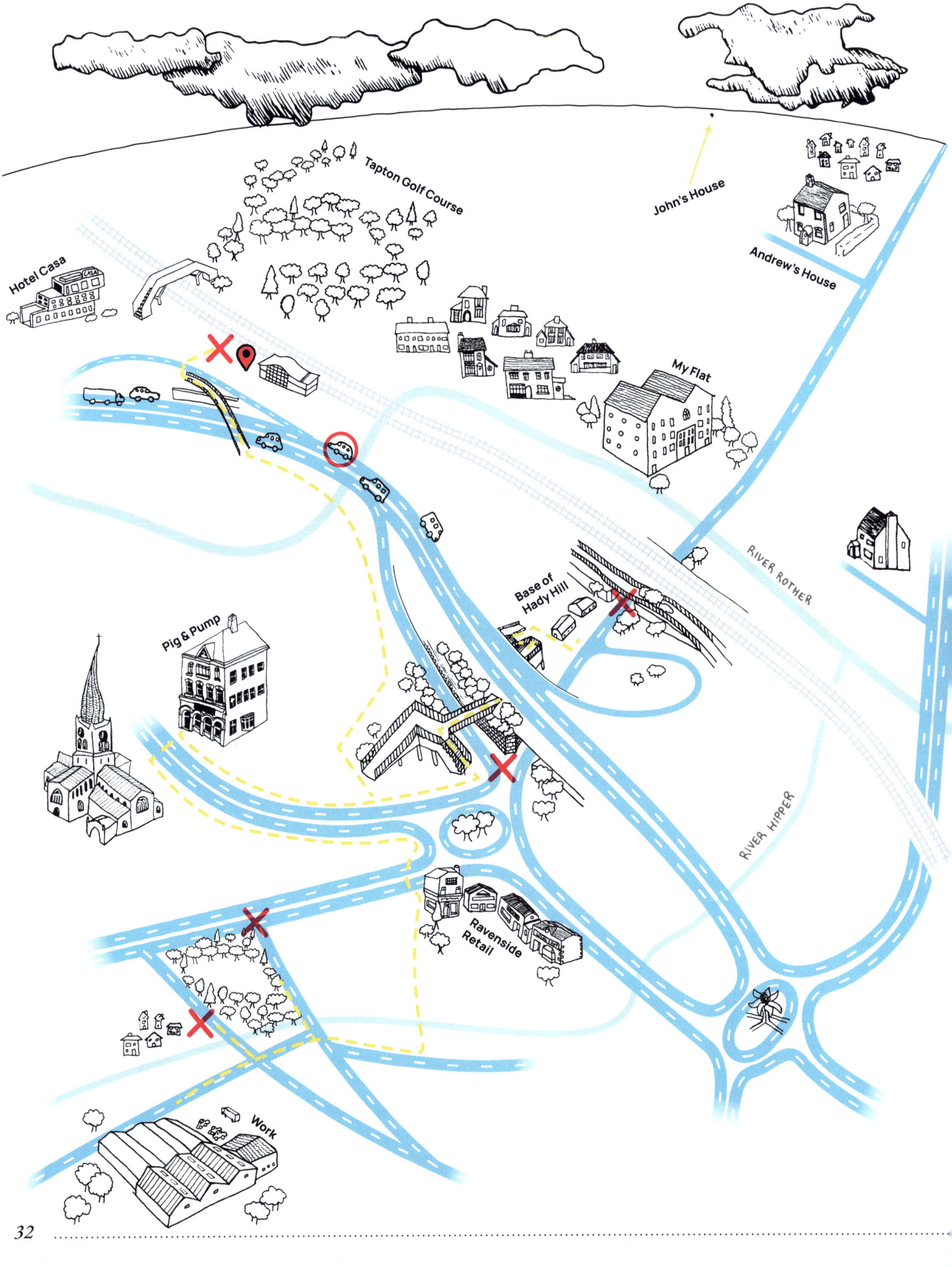
Tapton Golf Course
John's House
Andrew's House
Hotel Casa
My Flat
RIVER ROTHER
Base of
Hady Hill
Pig & Pump
RIVER HIPPER
Ravenside
Retail
Work

Returning to Chesterfield, I'm glad we didn't try to drive home that day or attempt to go through any of the areas with rapids in them.

Anyone who tried to cross or 'swim' through the water next to the railings of Crow Lane would have surely met their end. Attempting to drive through would also have been a terrible idea. If you find yourself in similar circumstances, be sensible and find an alternative way around. It's not worth risking your life.

It's often hard to capture rain falling in photographs; without any backlight, it has an annoying tendency to disappear. So as you look through this book you might think: It's not even raining. Well, I direct your attention to the surface of the water. Broken into hundreds of ripples due to the constant drizzle driving into it. Now imagine walking through this for hours. It was our current reality.

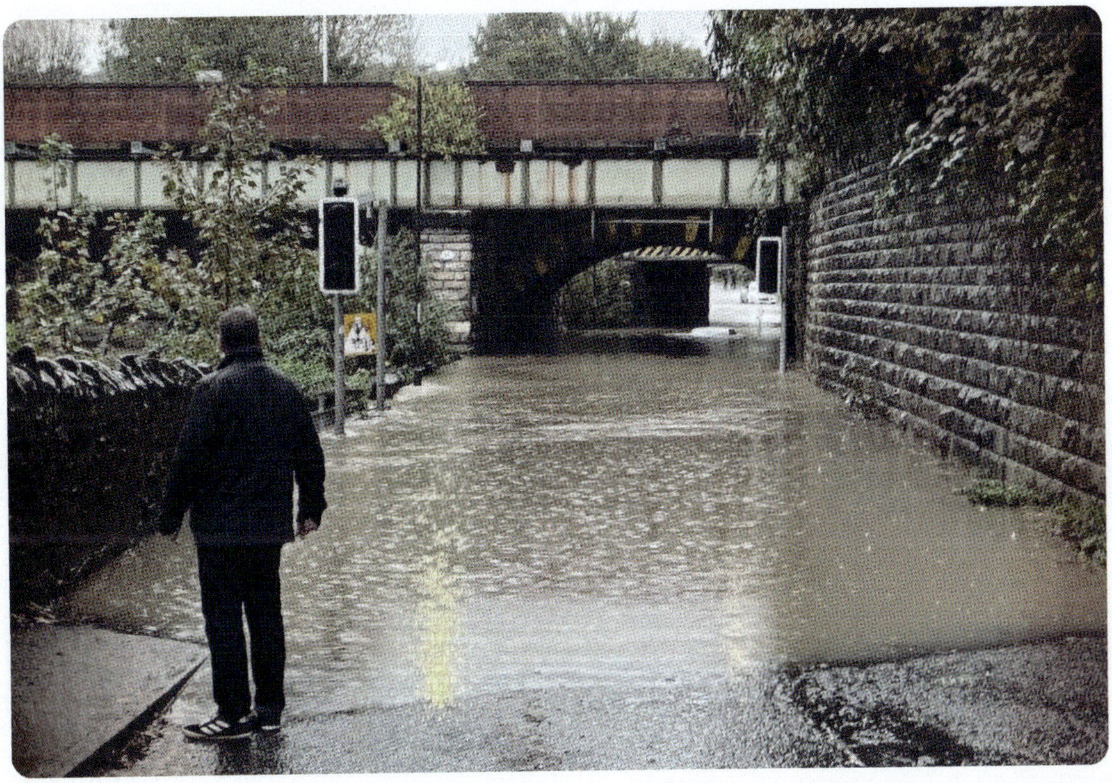

The gravity and severity of the situation made itself felt to all three of us. We had long since passed mere inconvenience and had entered into dangerous and risky territory. It would have been easy to get brought down by the situation. The world was gloomy and dark grey, surrounded by murky brown water with rubbish floating around. Every path we tried was blocked. The water levels seemed to still be rising. Unrelenting rain soaked us, removing all warmth. Would we ever make it home or were we trapped?

We could have *easily given up* hope,

but this **isn't that type of book**,

and I'm **not that kind of person**.

Instead, I took some photos and considered alternative plans. Plan F (I think we had by then abandoned plans A to E) would be staying in a hotel in central Chesterfield for the night. However, given the current devastation, I assumed these would be filled with people whose homes had flooded. It's fortunate there are a fair few hotels in Chesterfield. Failing that, plan G, we could ask people we know who live in Chesterfield for help. I later found out that many people took up one of these options, especially if they were looking after young children. It makes sense as you wouldn't want them walking through flooded areas.

The final alternative, plan H, would be to head back to work, something that Andrew, John and I had joked about a couple of times as we were met with seemingly impassible flooded areas. Although a joke, it was a viable backup plan. I was confident that even if we got stuck in Chesterfield for the night, it wouldn't be too much of an issue.

By now it was almost 5pm, and Andrew suggested trying to go down Brimington Road. He mentioned that from there we could get onto the golf course and go round that way. John and I agreed. It's odd how different your planning becomes in these circumstances; you are forced to take routes that you would never normally consider. You start thinking along the lines of: How low is the water at this point? If the road is flooded here then it's likely that it will be there, too!

I will pause for a moment to say that I must sound like I know the geography of Chesterfield well; I don't. Andrew and John possessed knowledge of the area which provided options for ways around. If I had been on my own, I'm not sure I would have made it across Markham Road. A humbling reminder that people are stronger when working as a team.

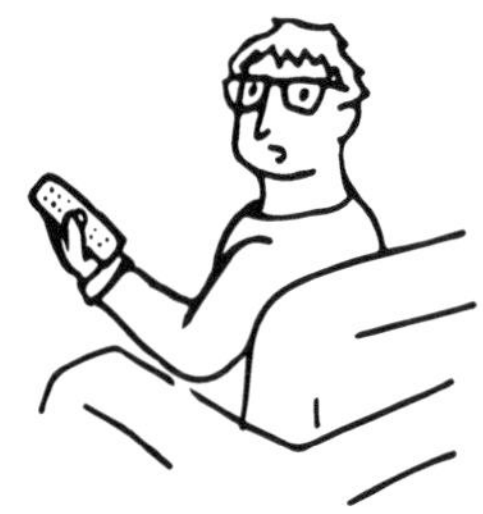

Doubling back, we turned right at the train station onto Brimington Road. As you might have guessed, it was flooded. *Ugh, this was frustrating*. I had come to expect it at this point. However, we noticed that there were cars successfully going through and it was certainly the shallowest water I had seen that day on any flooded road. It was probably only around 10–20cm deep. More importantly for us though, a number of pedestrians were making the crossing.

'I think we'll be able to get across here,' said Andrew, turning towards John and me. We nodded in agreement. Without hesitation, John charged forward, splashing water with his determined strides. It brought a smile to my face seeing him finally able to 'swim'. I think he enjoyed being able to splash around in the water. In all seriousness, this was our best option and we pushed our way through the water.

It was odd how, even amongst the disorder and chaos of the situation, somehow there was a calm order to everyone making the crossing. For part of the path, a handrail provided support and extra stability, useful when you can't see what you're standing on. It's all too easy to 'cockle over' (as they say in Hull) a kerb or pothole. And with transport as bad as it was, I wouldn't want to have to figure out how to get to hospital. A sense of relief hung in the air, and I wondered how many blocked crossings others had faced. For that matter, how many had we? By my count it was five.

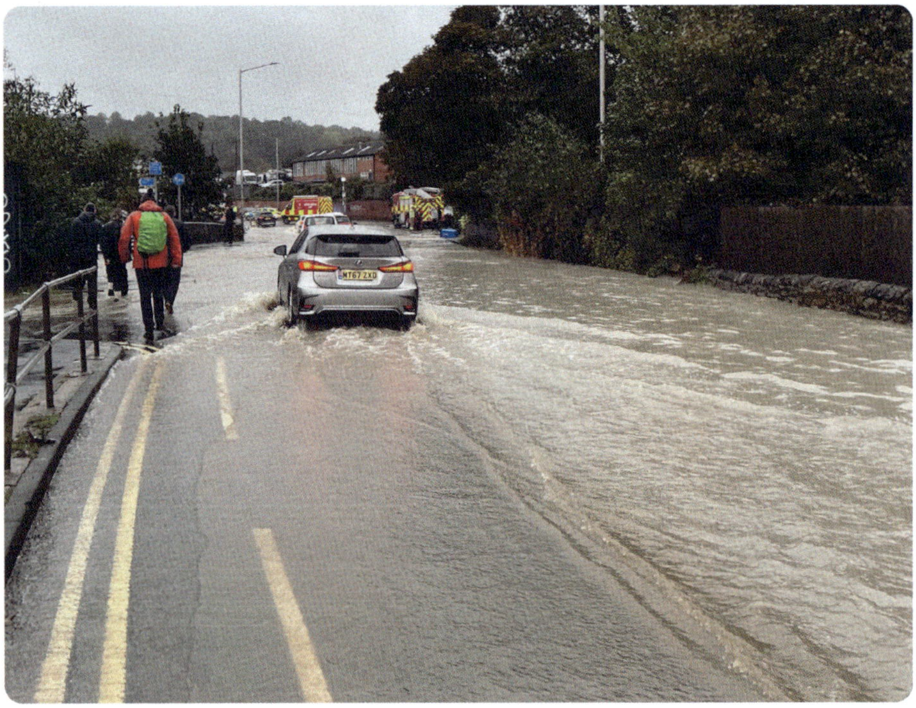

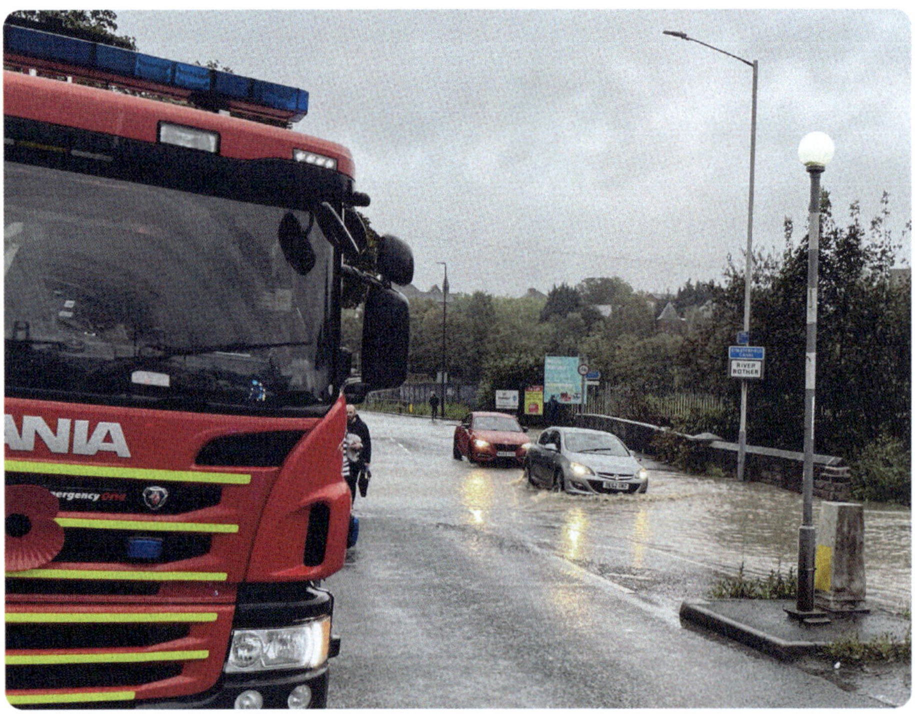
ANIA
RIVER ROTHER

The flood crept up on us by stealth; it was never noisy, and everywhere we travelled that day had a subdued quiet about it. Even when there were a lot of people around, it was quiet. It makes me wonder if everyone was in their own heads, deep in thought, thinking where they should go, what to do next, and how to deal with this unprecedented challenge.

There was a fire engine at the other side of this flooded road. It was hard to tell exactly what was going on, and I never stopped to ask them, but I'm assuming they were there to help residents evacuate and to monitor the situation. Slightly further up there were a couple of police cars. I found it interesting that they had decided not to block off this road too, but I was glad they didn't.

We crossed onto the right hand side of the road next to the fire engine. After successfully making it through, I turned and quickly took a photo of the flooded houses in Tapton Terrace. I did not know at the time that the owner of one of these houses was 83 year-old Maureen Gilbert who sadly died in the flood. I don't know for certain, but given the water level, it is likely she had already passed away by the time we walked by.

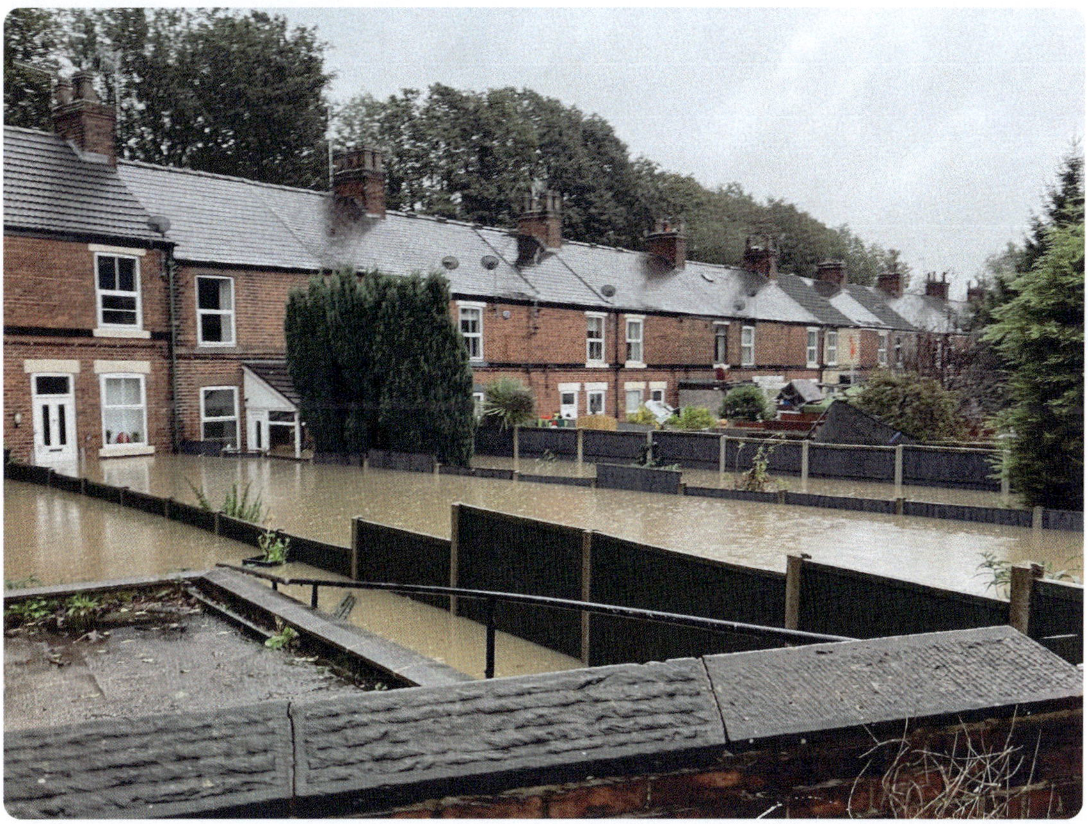

Flooded houses in Tapton Terrace.

Continuing down Brimington Road, we reached the footbridge over the railway onto Tapton Park Golf Course. We then made use of the trees and shrubbery surrounding the golf course for a bathroom break, before reconvening to figure out which way we needed to go.

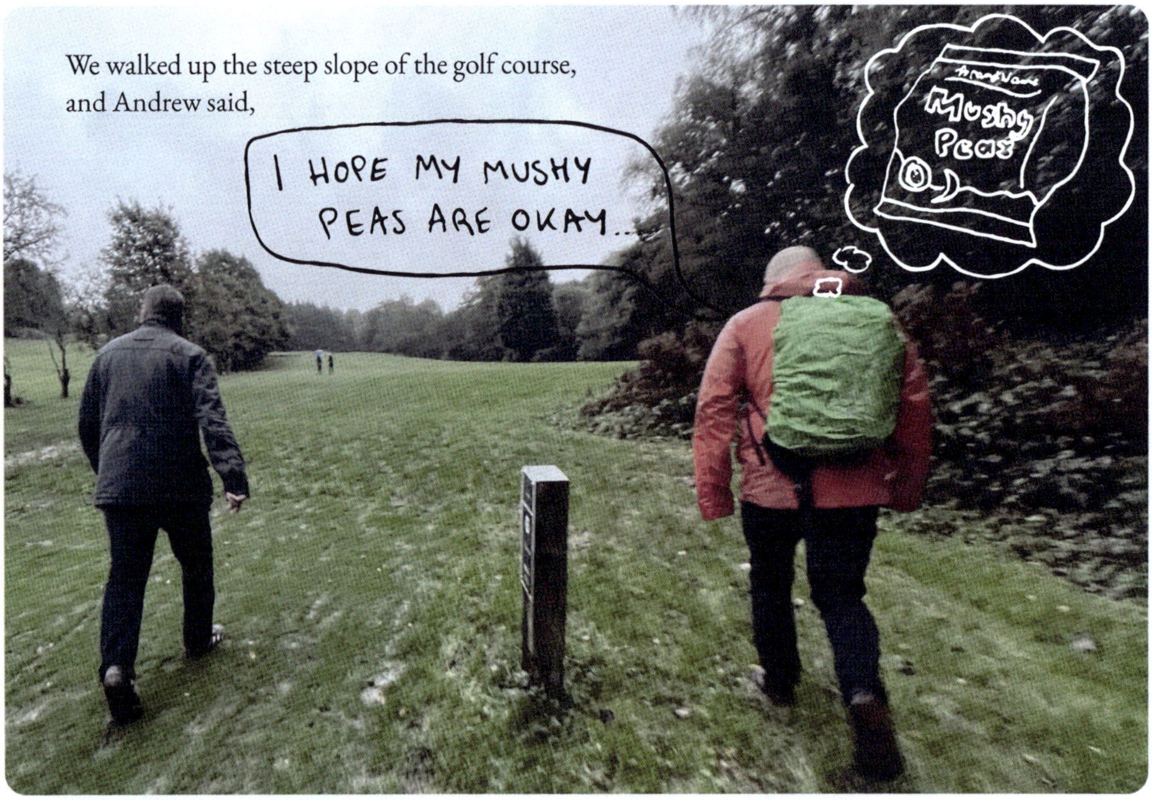

The same ones that had been sitting at the bottom of his bag throughout our journey. If they weren't mushy before, they certainly were now! We all had a little laugh about this.

Eventually, the ground started to level off and I turned around to take a photo of Andrew as he crested the hill. You can see the drizzle hanging like a mist over Chesterfield in the background. For the first time since setting off, we felt like we had got somewhere. We had journeyed beyond the impassible water divides that had fractured Chesterfield's roads.

It may sound strange, given the circumstances, but I was quite happy on that hill. As a unit we had overcome some incredible obstacles that day. I remember telling Andrew and John that this was a crazy adventure and laughing about it. I mean what else could you do?

‘My feet are soaked,’ said John, stamping on the sodden ground, his shoes making a squelching noise.

‘Mine, too,’ Andrew added. ‘Have been for ages.’

Naturally, I took this opportunity to share how dry my feet were, which, of course, was met with some envy.

‘Yeah, it was a good idea to wear those,’ Andrew said, pointing wistfully at my wellies.

Even John, who hadn’t been in the greatest of moods, perked up slightly. Admittedly, he had to go all the way to Shirebrook and, while mine and Andrew’s journeys were almost over, his was only halfway complete.

‘Maybe we shouldn’t have stayed so long at the pub,’ John said ruefully.

We passed a number of people on the golf course. I hadn’t previously spent a great deal of time walking across it, but I imagine there were significantly more than you would usually expect. Some were wearing makeshift bin bag ponchos, some wearing jackets and others wielding umbrellas. Regardless, each one of them was soaked.

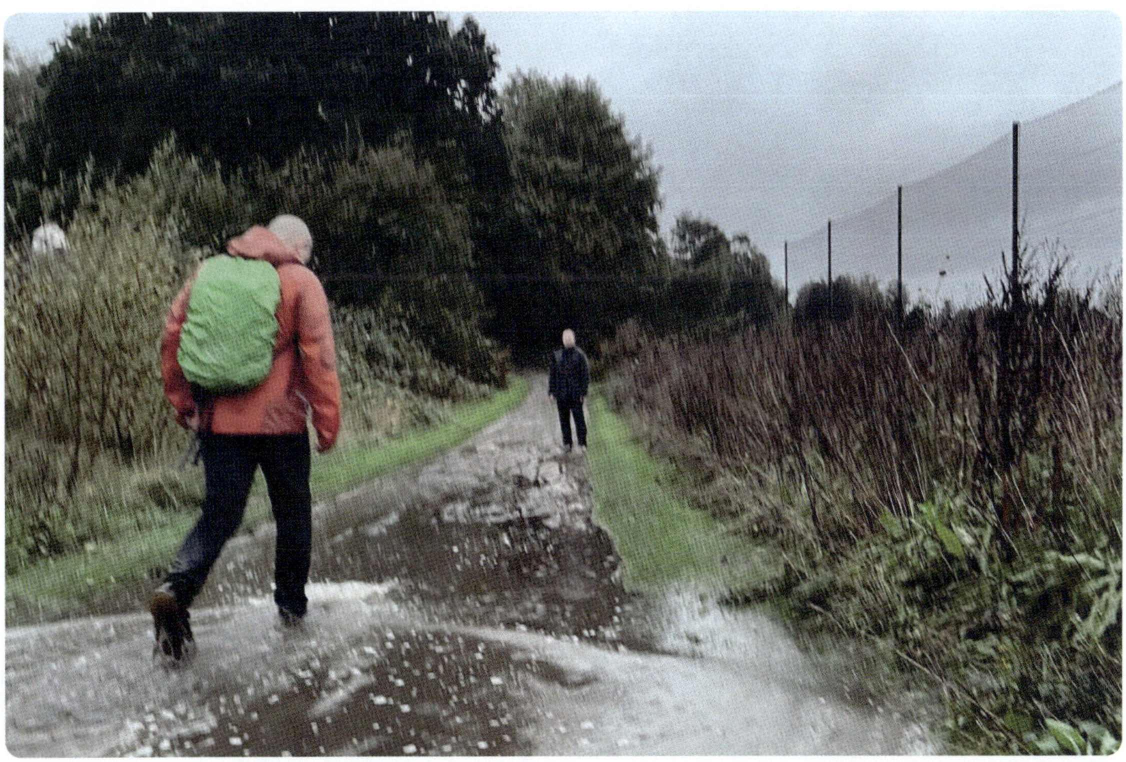

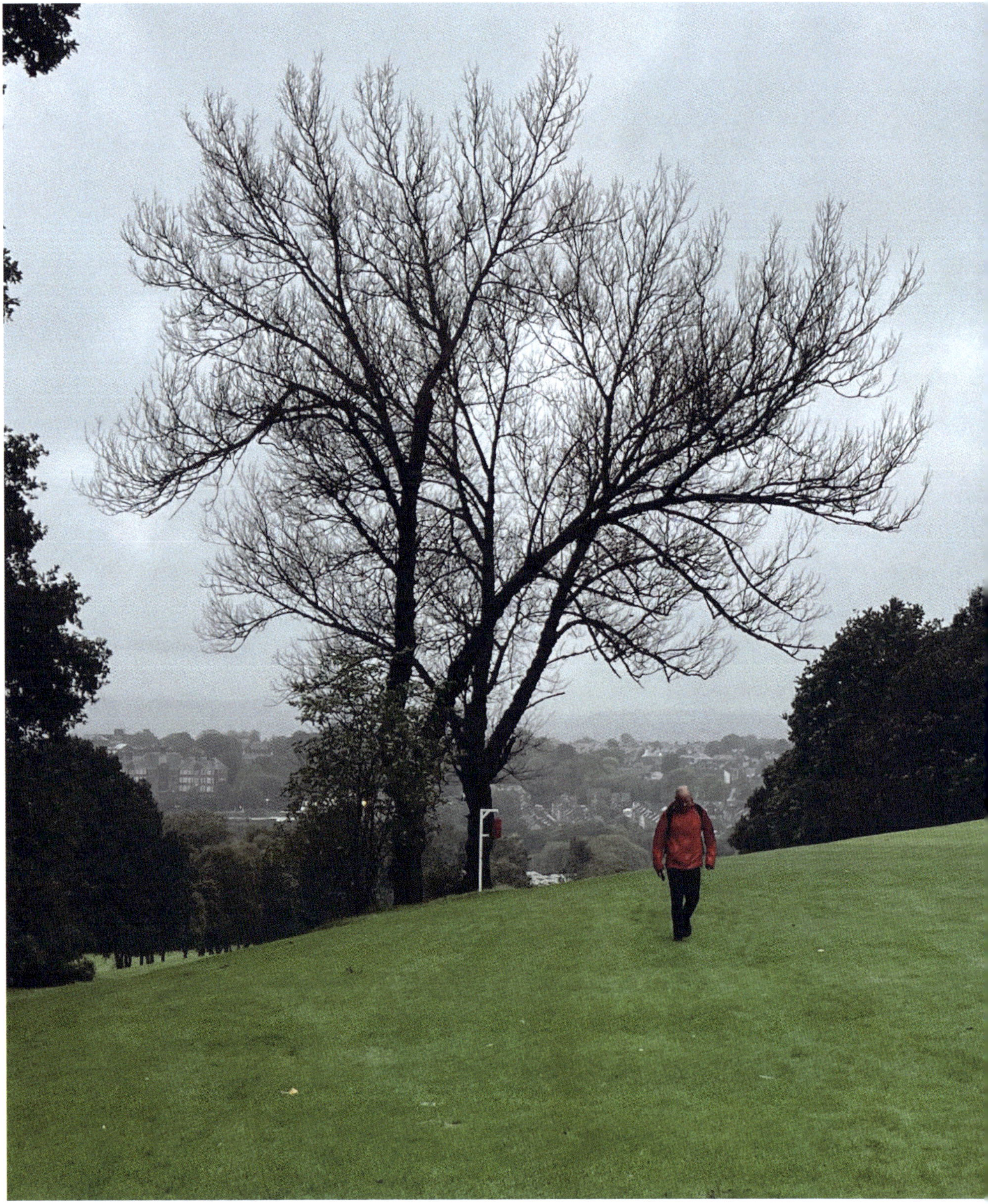

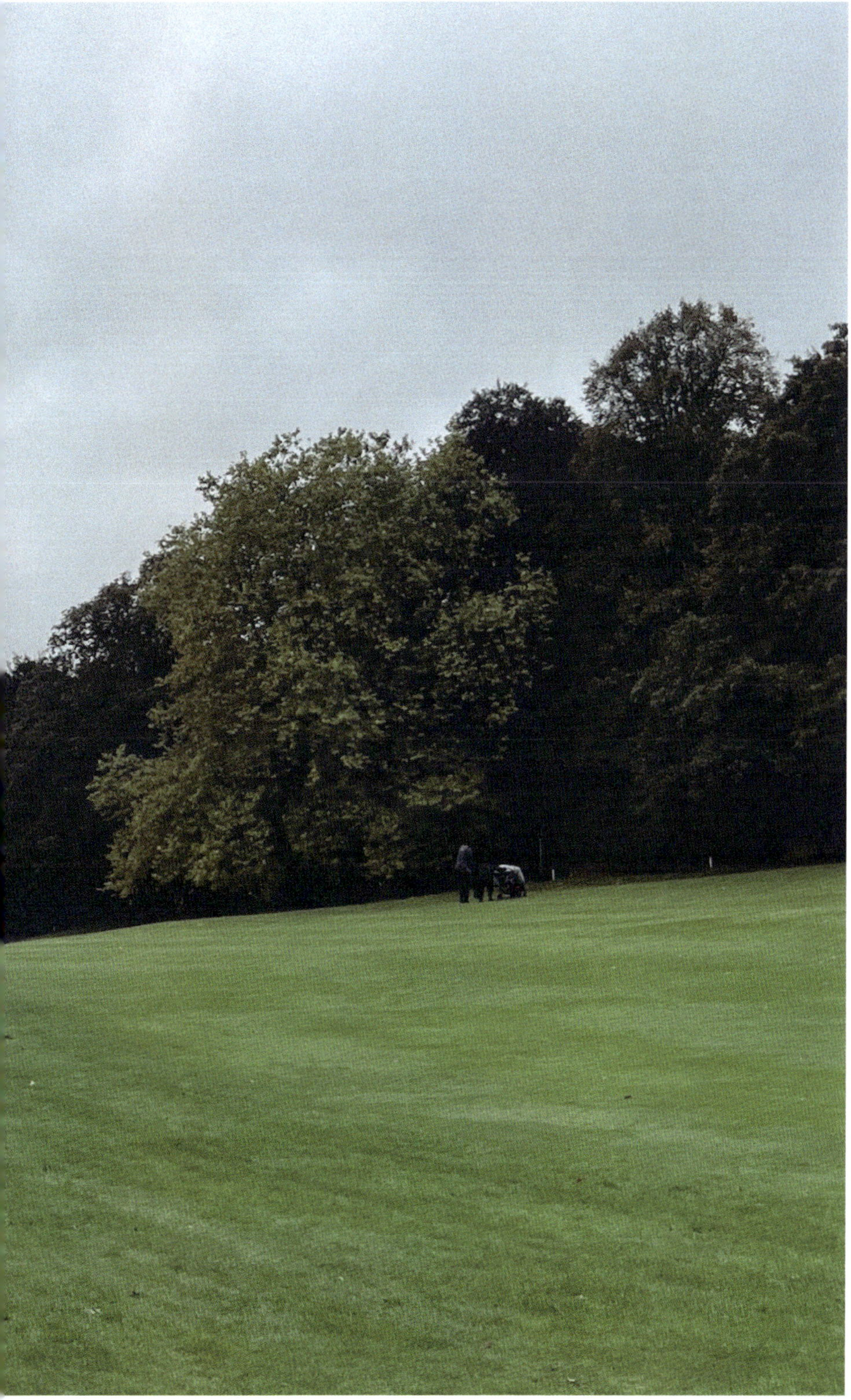

None of us were familiar with the layout of the golf course. We figured our best option was to head to the clubhouse, as this connected to the roads we needed to reach. We consulted the GPS on our phones and took a haphazard route towards it. As a result we overshot, so we had to go around the back of the driving range.

Once again, we encountered a flooded pathway. Andrew and I discussed if there was another way around. It didn't look particularly bad, but we also wanted to ensure it was the correct way to go. After all, you wouldn't want to get wet only to discover you'd gone the wrong way and have to go through it again.

In the meantime, John had approached a couple of ladies standing on the dry embankment, who were lost. According to John, they were trying to get to a rave! I know it sounds bonkers, right? If I'd have known this at the time, I'd have asked them about it, but we only found out from John afterwards.

Then, without warning, John charged through the water, splashing everyone. Andrew and I chuckled. To be honest, for me it made no difference, though it would result in wet feet again for Andrew and John. They both ended up throwing away the shoes they were wearing that day due to them being covered in muck and full of silt. As it happened, it was the right way to go, and we all splashed through.

The two women followed our group back up the path, unsure of where they needed to go. Andrew advised them on the best way around, and we parted ways. I wonder if they made it to that rave?

Eventually, we made it to the clubhouse. Andrew said, 'This is where we split up. John and I will take the top path, and you can follow that down to pick up Crow Lane behind the train station.' He pointed in the direction I should go. 'Give me a call if you have any problems.'

I said goodbye and wished them both good luck, before we parted ways.

I had only been walking for a minute or so before being stopped by a series of people in small groups of two or three, all walking in a convoy. It was like a 'bus' of people without the actual bus! They asked me for directions and information on how to get to central Chesterfield, and about what was and wasn't closed. I gave the best advice I could, based on my experiences. This involved me having to think of our route in reverse and explaining all the areas I knew were definitely blocked.

The last woman I spoke to asked me where I was heading, and it transpired she lived on the ground floor of a block of flats across the road from mine. She explained that her flat was already flooded and under a couple of inches of water.

Given the sights I had seen that day, I wasn't surprised, and I had come to realise my flat had probably been flooded to some extent. But hearing it confirmed out loud made it all the more real. But I had come this far on the journey and knew it was something I had to see for myself.

I think everyone would want to see for themselves. Even if she had shown me video evidence and photos, I'd still have gone. I didn't debate it for a second; I just knew that's what I was going to do. Besides, it didn't sound like that much water. I wished the lady and the group luck on their journey and continued on. I now wonder what happened to those people and how badly they were affected in the months afterwards.

Evidently, Andrew and John had seen this exchange from slightly higher up on the hill, and Andrew rang me to ask if everything was okay. I explained that I had been giving directions to people about the route we had just taken, but purposefully didn't mention what the lady had said about the flats already being flooded. He told me to give him a ring if there were any problems when I reached home. I suspect he realised the truth of the situation.

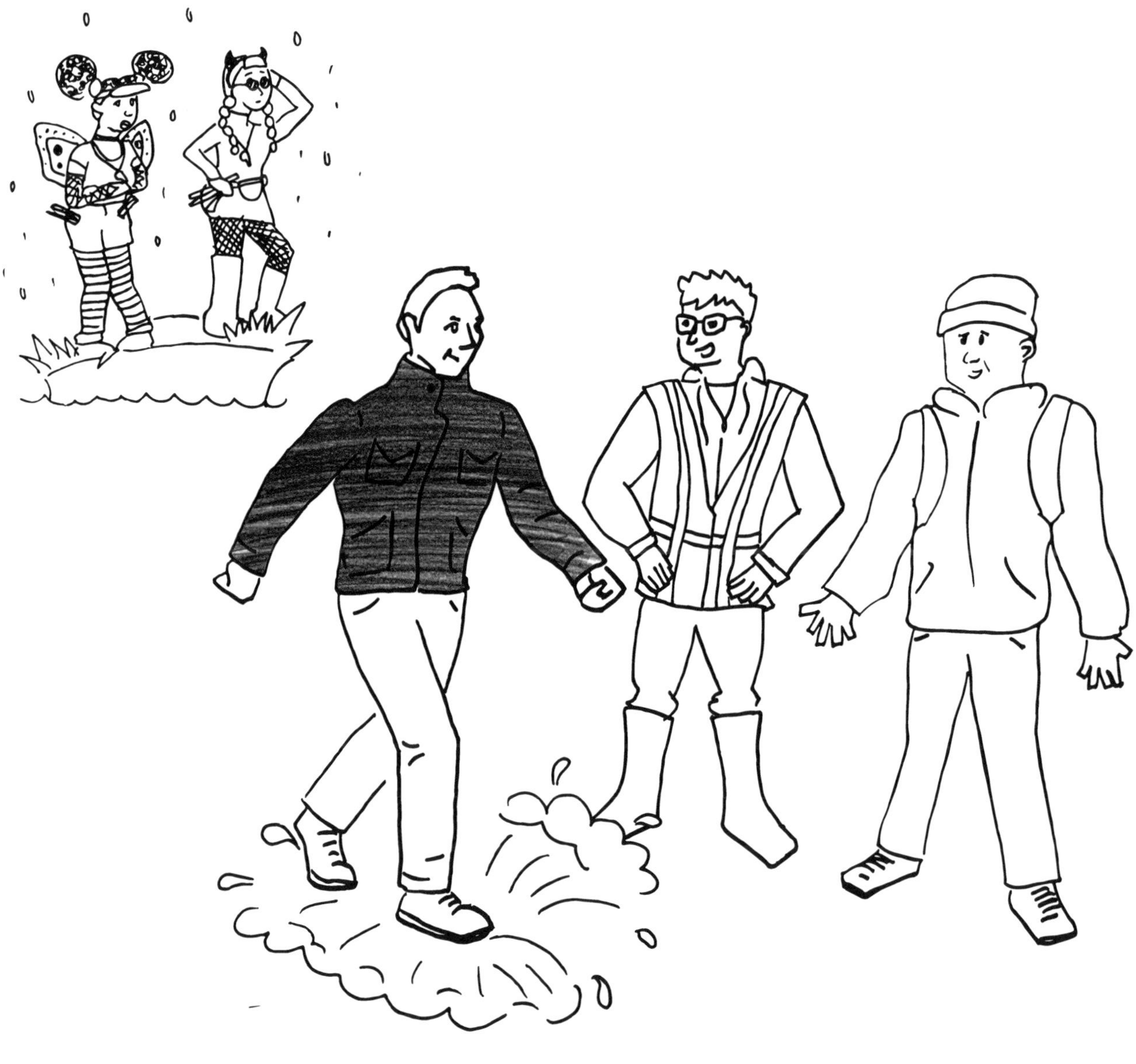

John & Andrew's Story

John and Andrew continued to the top of Crow Lane which leads onto Wetlands Lane, Westmoor Road, Eastmoor Road and Blacksmith Lane, arriving in Calow. Andrew and John split here at around 6.15pm. Andrew made it home shortly after. Andrew's commute had taken around four hours and twenty-five minutes.

John continued on the A632. A passerby in a car informed him that it was flooded and impassible at Arkwright, so he took a detour. I'm surprised he didn't attempt to swim! So, John took Sutton Lane to Palterton Lane across the bridge on the M1 joining Carr Lane on the other side, where he made it to Palterton.

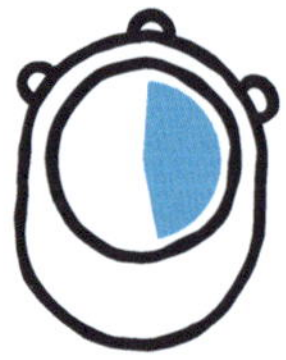

It had long since turned dark, while John was wandering around, and he described it as an eerie night with the moon lighting the sky so you could see without a torch, and the moonlight reflecting off the surface water. John's wife, Angela, managed to pick him up from Palterton and take him back home to Shirebrook. John arrived at around 8.15pm, after the longest commute out of all of us that day, at an impressive six and a half hours.

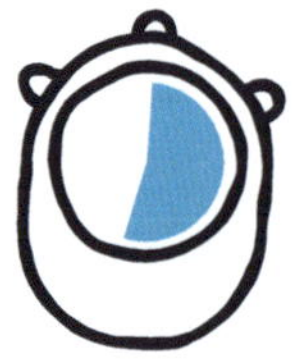

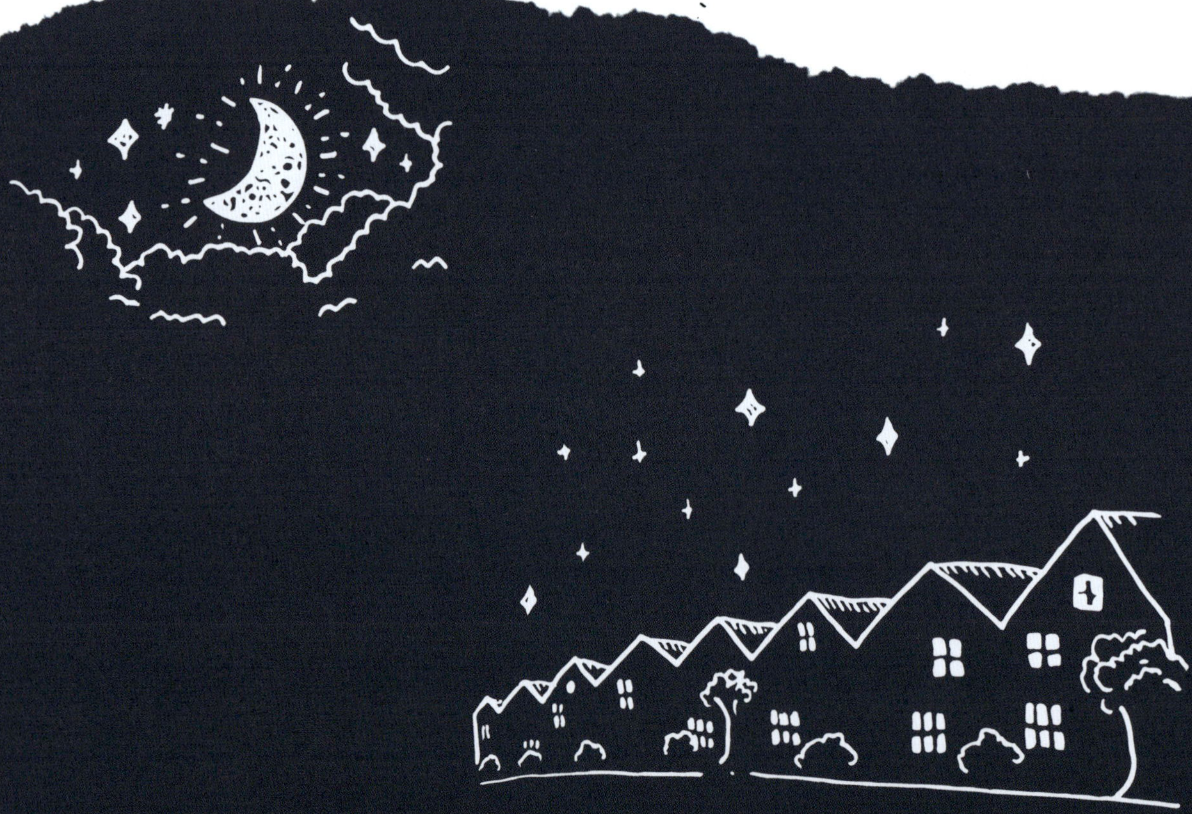

Joe's Story Continued

Meanwhile, I joined Crow Lane on the eastern side of the River Rother, the same road we had tried to get onto about forty-five minutes earlier, next to the train station on the western side of the river.

This was the first time I had been alone with my thoughts since I had started my day. I remember chuckling to myself about the absurdity of this situation. 'How did I get here?' I asked myself.

Back in 2020, I moved to Chesterfield from my hometown in Hull during the Covid-19 pandemic, having managed to secure a role at the factory as a graduate process engineer. I was excited about this opportunity, as I had had no fewer than 100 failed applications at that point. This is no exaggeration either; I have the spreadsheet to prove it!

Having spent two good years at the factory, I was offered the chance to become a chemical engineer at another company. This is what I had originally studied to become, so I decided to give this a go in 2022. As a result I left Chesterfield, and the factory, for just over a year. I hated it.

It was not a fun experience, but I don't regret it as it taught me a great deal about what I did and didn't want from life. At the year mark, I knew I had given this a fair go and it hadn't worked out. Luckily, I saw an advert for my current position back at my old factory and decided to take a chance.

You can guess what happened from the fact I live here now. It wasn't ever lost on me how incredibly lucky I was to have a role available when I needed it, and one that I was also excited about.

For the first time, I could afford to rent my own flat instead of living in a house share. This was an incredibly exciting prospect for me as, since the age of eighteen, I had shared with multiple people in order to pay the rent.

I almost didn't get my flat; when I first enquired about it someone had already applied and been accepted by the landlord pending reference checks. As it happened, they didn't pass the requirements and I was next in line to be offered a viewing.

I can clearly recall the day I was first shown around flat 36, which I would later call mine. The pretty blonde estate agent's high heels clicked on the laminate floors as she walked through the rooms with me. Beautiful twelve-foot ceilings with massive windows and exposed brick. The old foundry was certainly full of character, and I thought it was fantastic.

The estate agent's office was located in the town centre. I had been accepted as a tenant and had to go there to sign the paperwork and deal with the required admin. That's when I was asked the question: 'Do you want contents insurance? We can get you a good deal with a company if you are interested.'

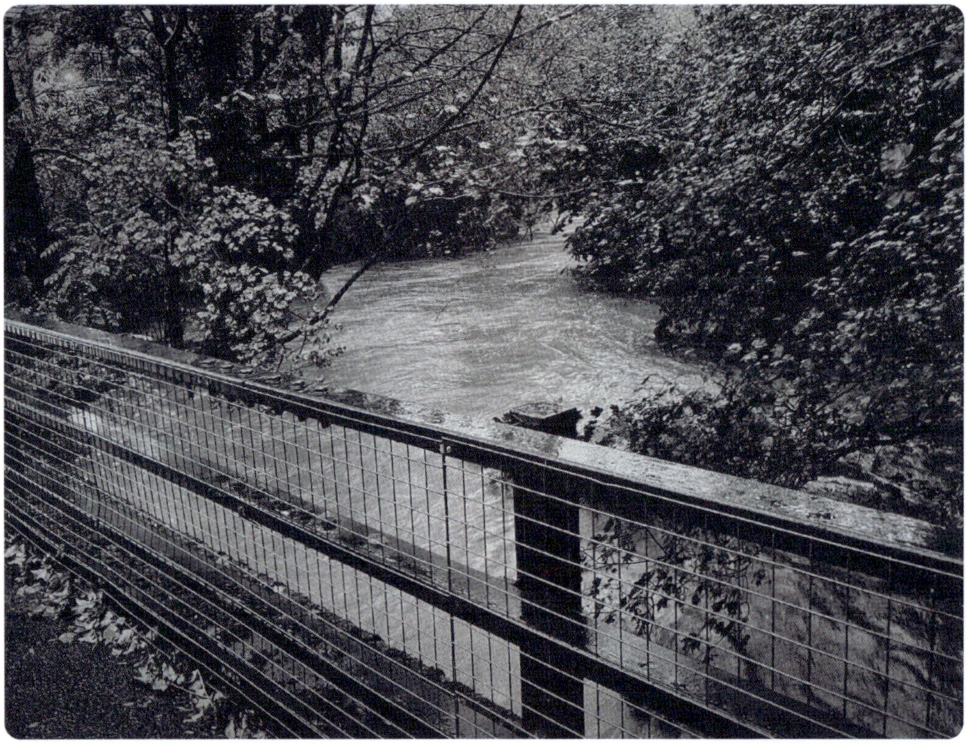

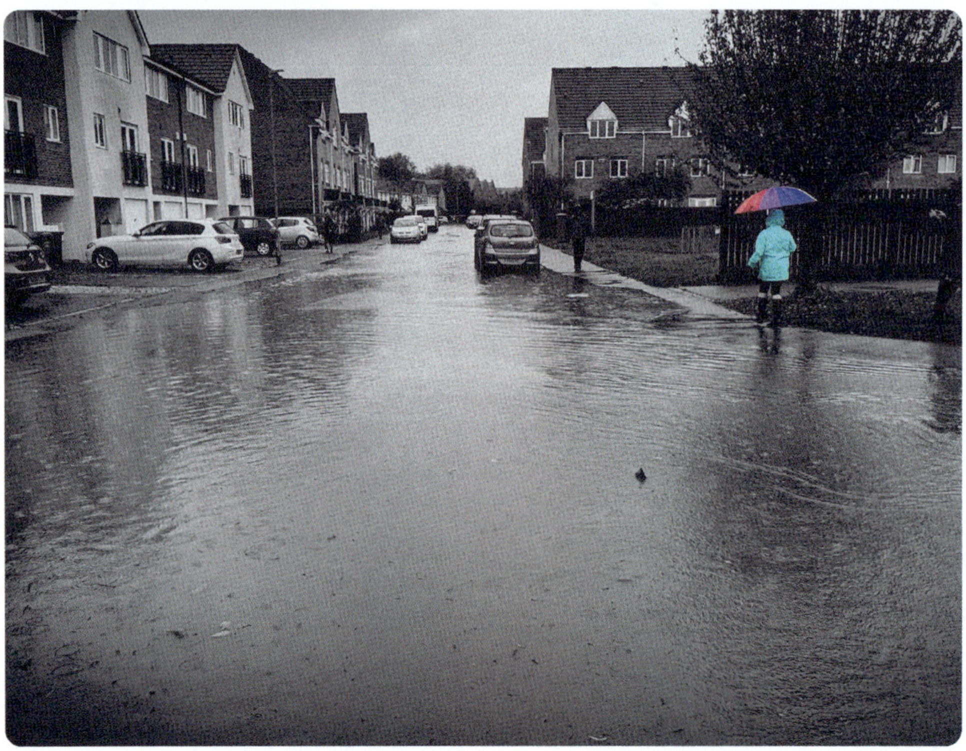

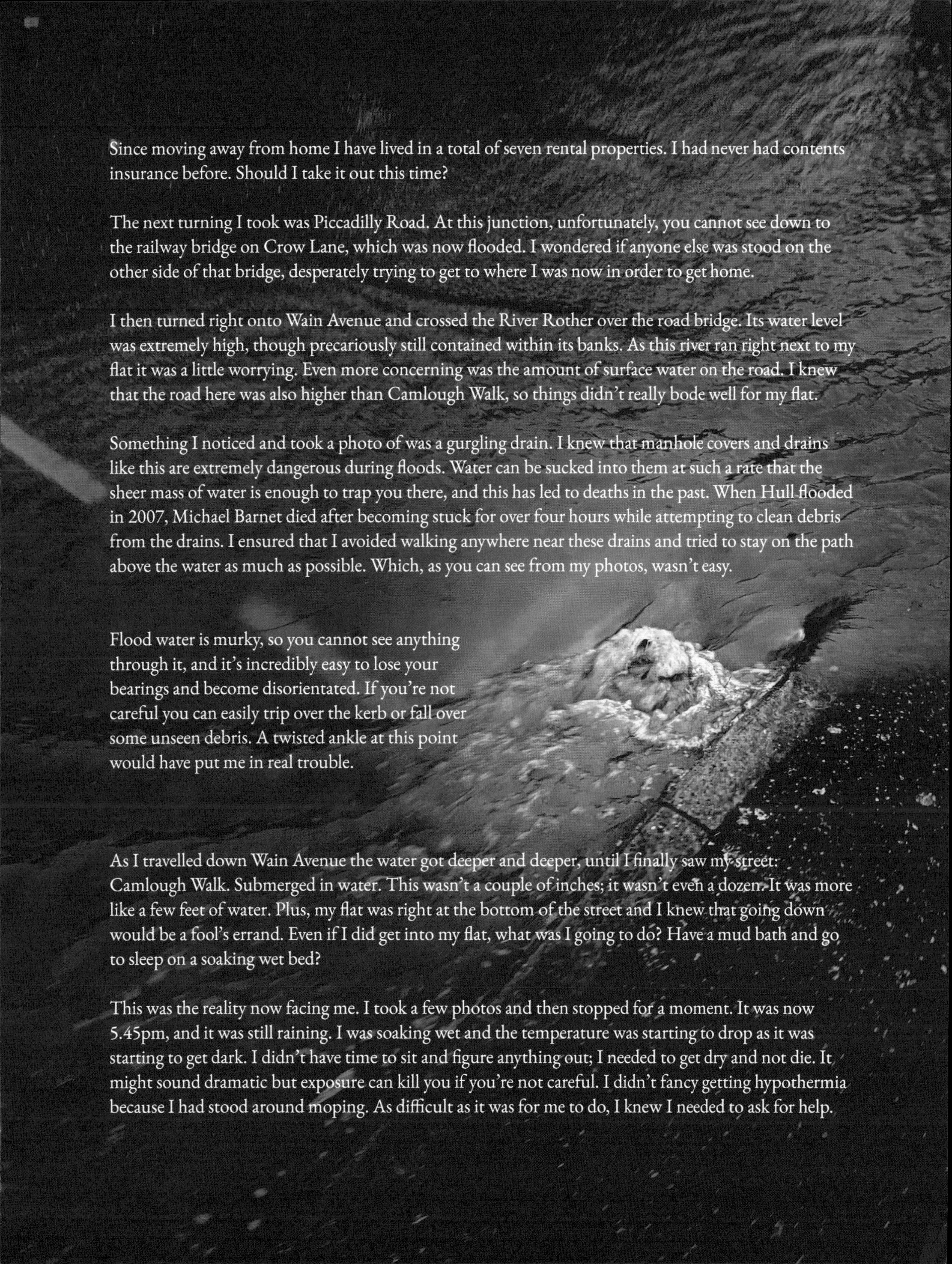

Since moving away from home I have lived in a total of seven rental properties. I had never had contents insurance before. Should I take it out this time?

The next turning I took was Piccadilly Road. At this junction, unfortunately, you cannot see down to the railway bridge on Crow Lane, which was now flooded. I wondered if anyone else was stood on the other side of that bridge, desperately trying to get to where I was now in order to get home.

I then turned right onto Wain Avenue and crossed the River Rother over the road bridge. Its water level was extremely high, though precariously still contained within its banks. As this river ran right next to my flat it was a little worrying. Even more concerning was the amount of surface water on the road. I knew that the road here was also higher than Camlough Walk, so things didn't really bode well for my flat.

Something I noticed and took a photo of was a gurgling drain. I knew that manhole covers and drains like this are extremely dangerous during floods. Water can be sucked into them at such a rate that the sheer mass of water is enough to trap you there, and this has led to deaths in the past. When Hull flooded in 2007, Michael Barnet died after becoming stuck for over four hours while attempting to clean debris from the drains. I ensured that I avoided walking anywhere near these drains and tried to stay on the path above the water as much as possible. Which, as you can see from my photos, wasn't easy.

Flood water is murky, so you cannot see anything through it, and it's incredibly easy to lose your bearings and become disorientated. If you're not careful you can easily trip over the kerb or fall over some unseen debris. A twisted ankle at this point would have put me in real trouble.

As I travelled down Wain Avenue the water got deeper and deeper, until I finally saw my street: Camlough Walk. Submerged in water. This wasn't a couple of inches; it wasn't even a dozen. It was more like a few feet of water. Plus, my flat was right at the bottom of the street and I knew that going down would be a fool's errand. Even if I did get into my flat, what was I going to do? Have a mud bath and go to sleep on a soaking wet bed?

This was the reality now facing me. I took a few photos and then stopped for a moment. It was now 5.45pm, and it was still raining. I was soaking wet and the temperature was starting to drop as it was starting to get dark. I didn't have time to sit and figure anything out; I needed to get dry and not die. It might sound dramatic but exposure can kill you if you're not careful. I didn't fancy getting hypothermia because I had stood around moping. As difficult as it was for me to do, I knew I needed to ask for help.

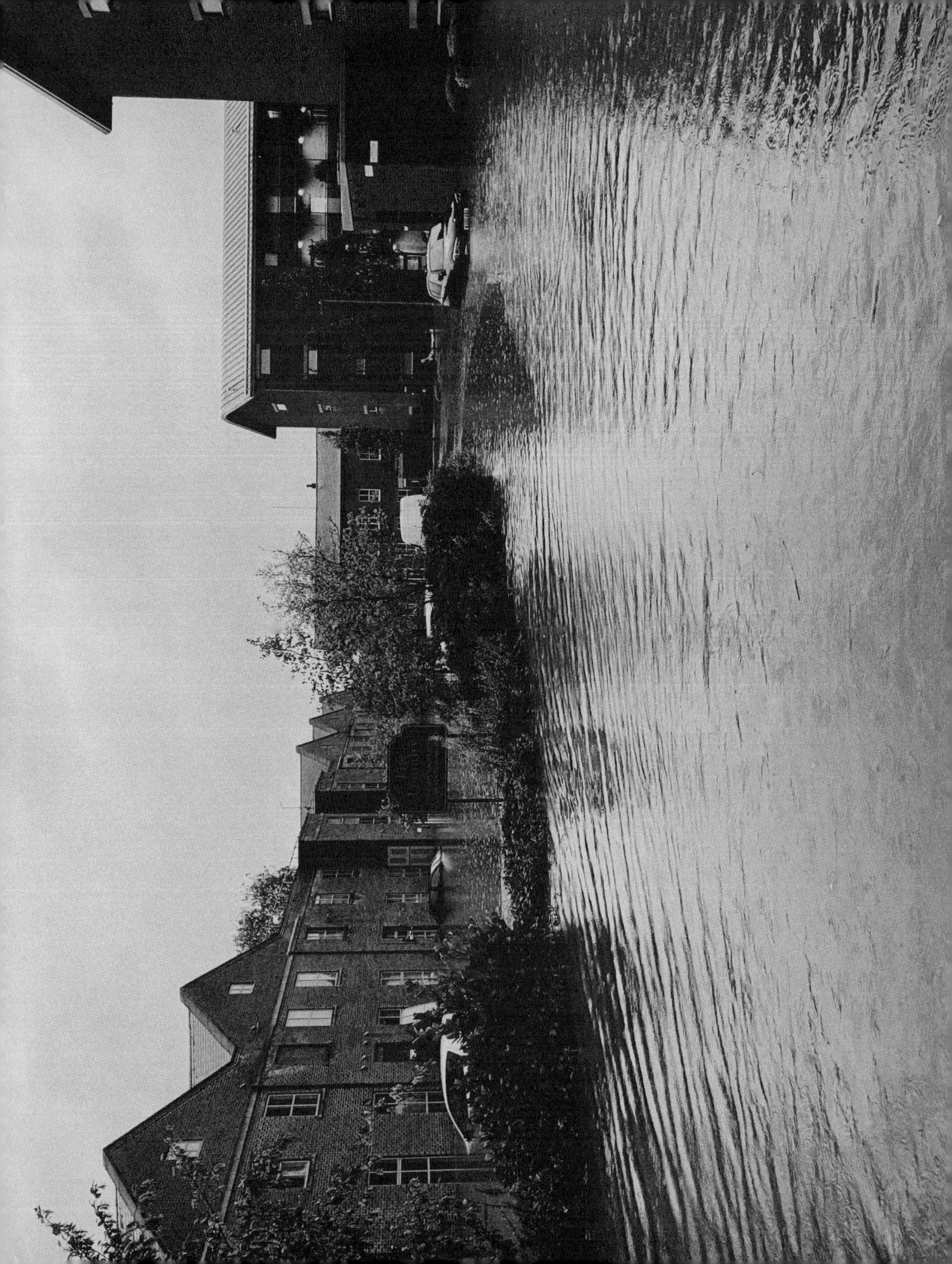

I rang Andrew and explained the situation and he kindly offered for me to stay at his house in Calow. He'd just made it back by the time I rang and told me the traffic was at a standstill, so I'd have to walk as it would be pointless Andrew driving to pick me up. It is about two miles uphill on foot, and takes about forty-five minutes. So I set off up Hady Hill to Andrew's.

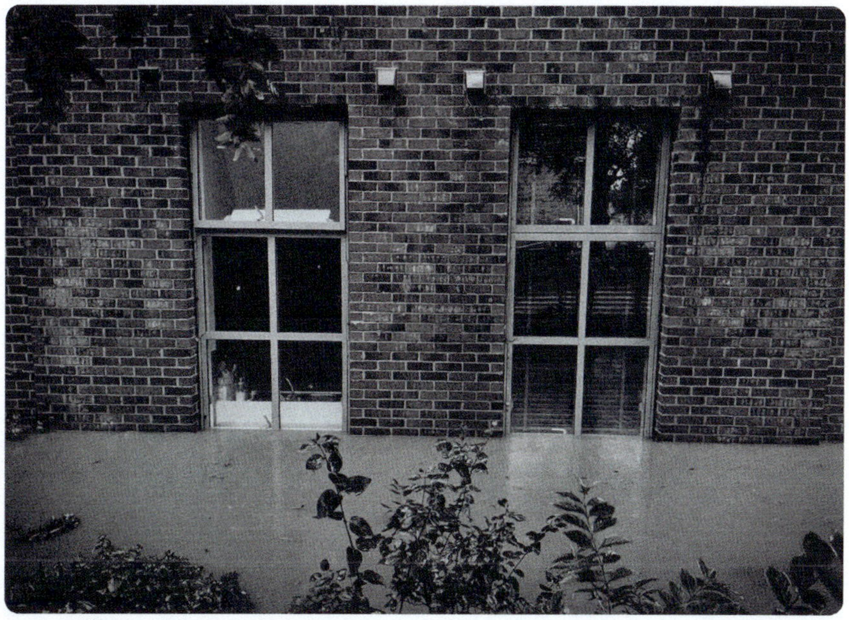

The first part of this journey is steep. By this point, my hands were cold and blood sugar low. This was by far the most mentally challenging section of the journey. The setbacks of the day and my recent discovery of a flooded flat weighed on my mind. I was technically now homeless, at least for tonight. Thinking like this wasn't going to help, so I decided to steel my resolve and push forward. My main focus was to keep putting one foot in front of the other and reaching Andrew's house.

I climbed Hady Hill, cresting its steep face. I gave a sigh of relief when the elevations ahead became less aggressive. It was then I noticed that the traffic near the hospital was heavy and barely moving. Clearly, walking was significantly faster than driving as I overtook every car.

Once past the hospital I decided to stop at a Co-op and purchase some water to drink. Ironic I know! This was only a brief pause before continuing on to Calow. I finally reached Andrew's house at around 7.00pm. My commute took about five hours and ten minutes.

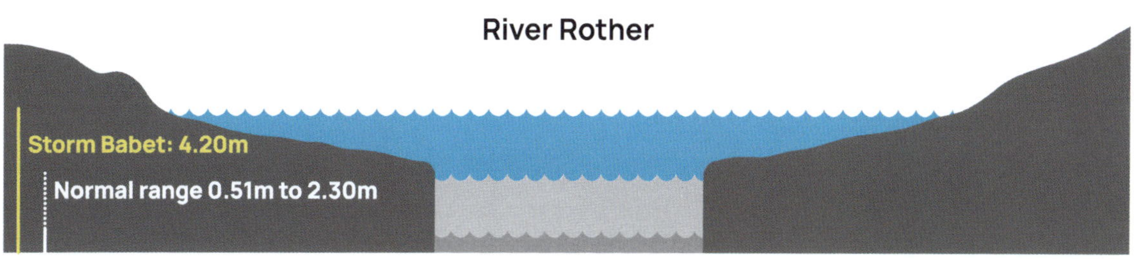

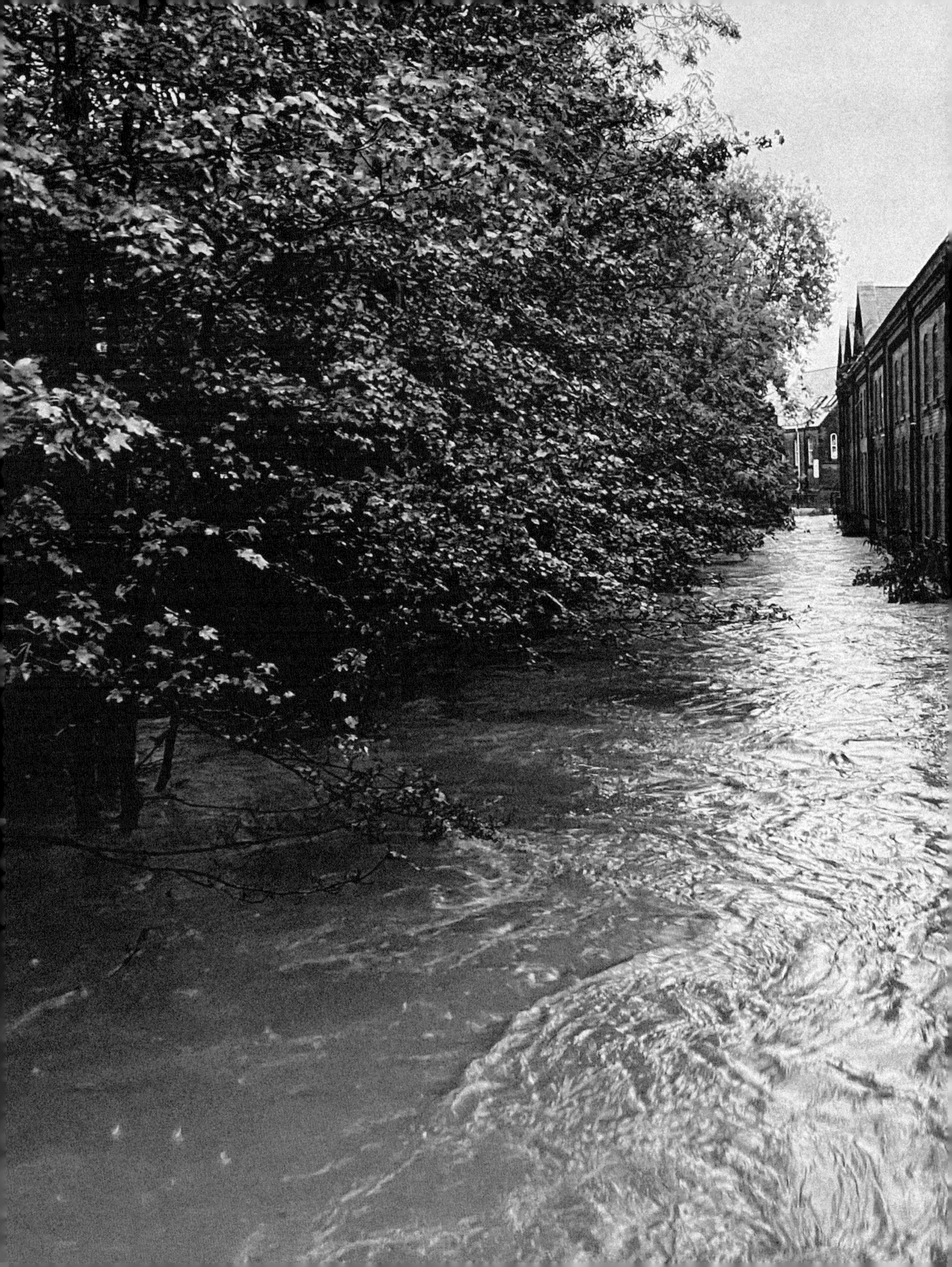

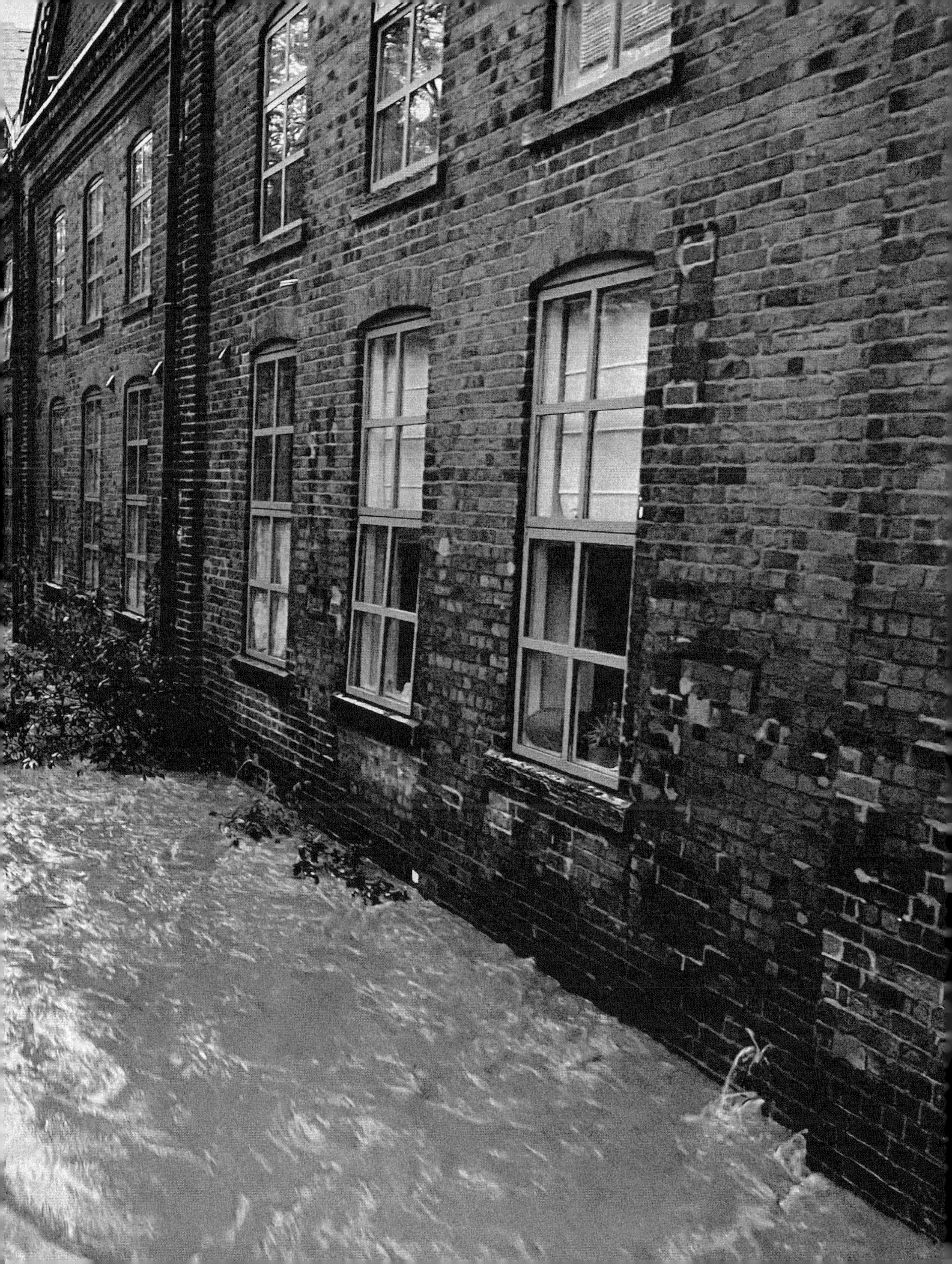

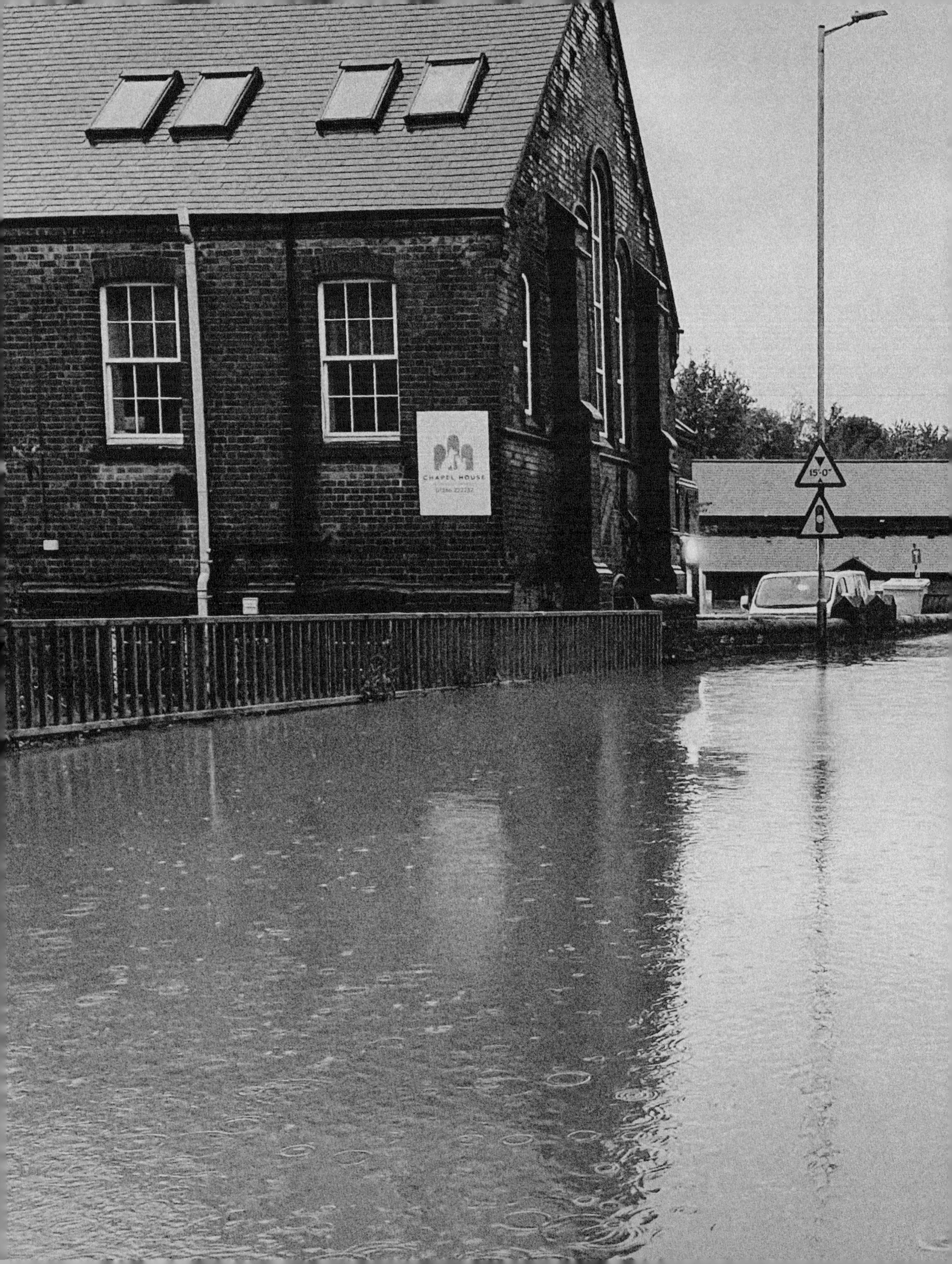
CHAPEL HOUSE
15'-0"

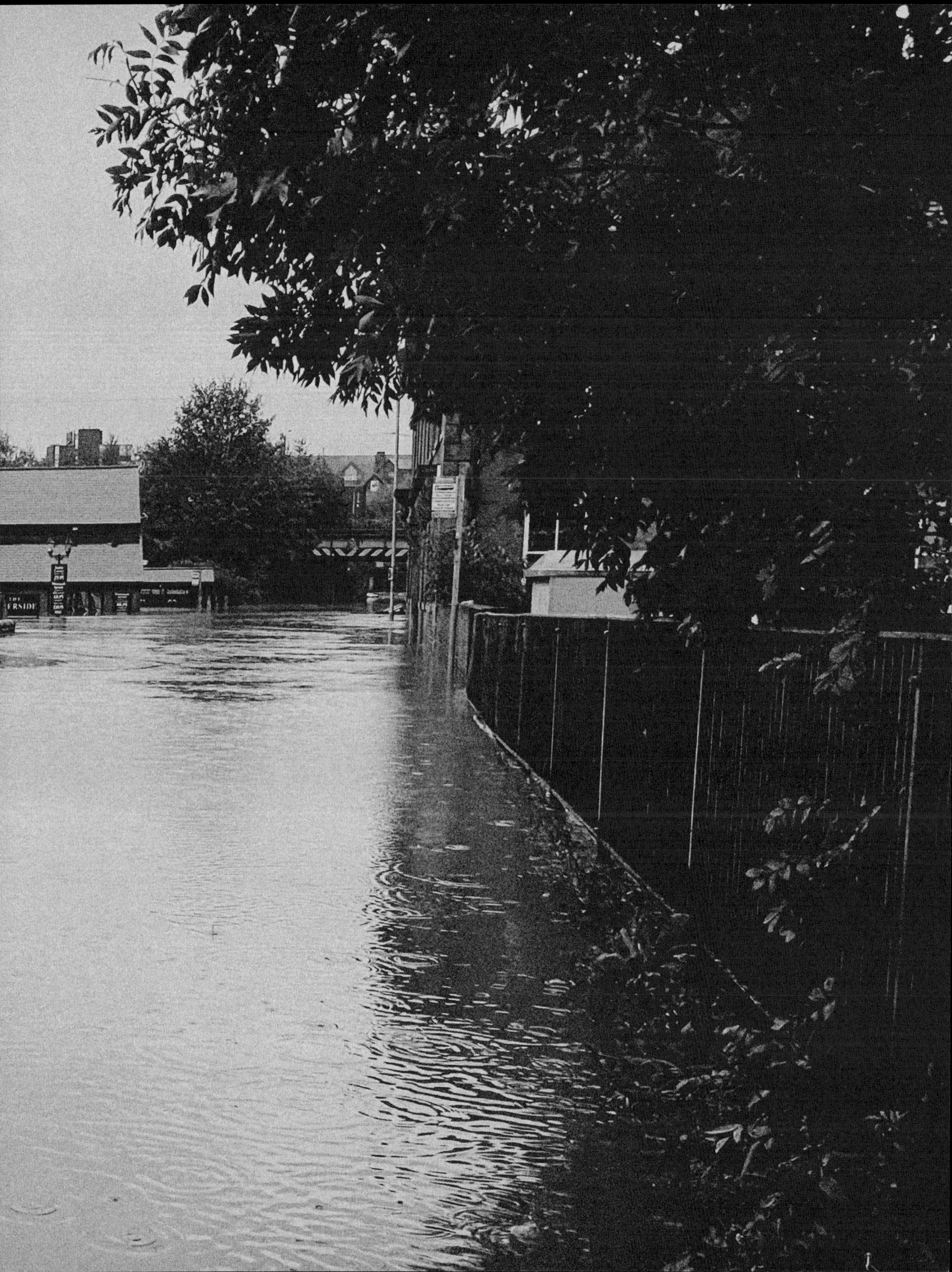

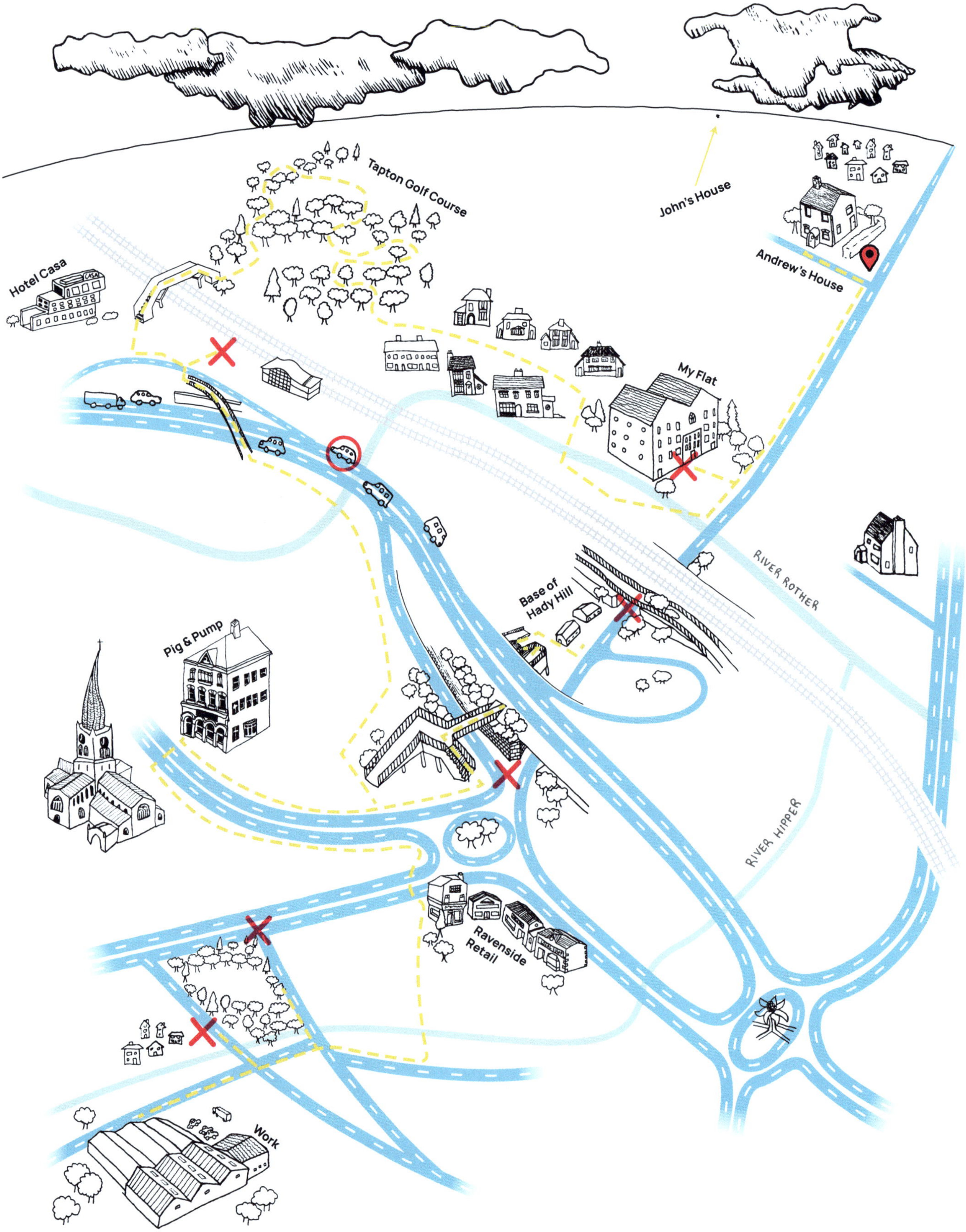
Tapton Golf Course
John's House
Hotel Casa
Andrew's House
My Flat
River Rother
Base of Hady Hill
Pig & Pump
River Hipper
Ravenside Retail
Work

I walked into Andrew's house absolutely drenched. If I'd have jumped into a swimming pool and got out, I'd have been equally soaked. There was literally a pool of water where I was standing in his kitchen. Andrew and his partner, Christina, were very kind, lending me dry clothes and setting up the world's most complicated shower for me to use. Christina was even kind enough to wash and dry my clothes.

I have never appreciated a warm shower more than at that moment. It seemed to melt away the cold, and restore my partially numb body back to life. Being able to change into dry clothes was another luxury.

I was also treated to a lovely home-cooked pie and the mushy peas Andrew had been carrying the entire time we were on our adventure. As good as they were, I did wonder if it was the journey that had made them mushy rather than them starting out that way. Andrew assures me that this was not the case, and the peas were always mushy! Although I didn't realise at first, Christina had given her slice of pie to me, which I was truly grateful for, as by now, I was extremely hungry.

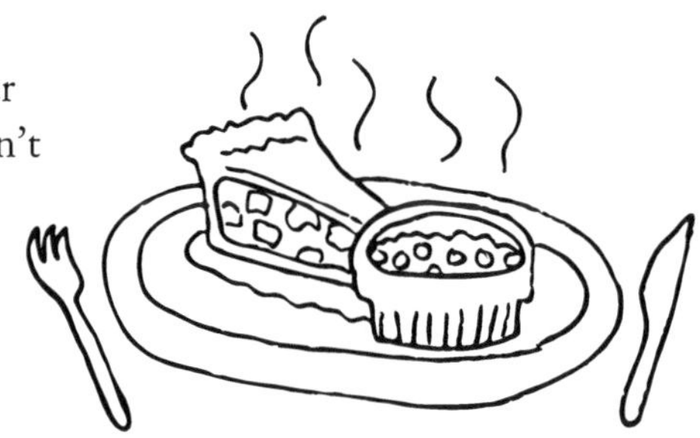

After eating, we sat in the kitchen where I drank Andrew's craft beer collection. By this point, my mood had significantly improved. I don't think there are many worse feelings then being cold and damp. There's a reason we use the phrase 'dampen your spirits'. I think mine certainly had been dampened, though had now recovered.

Andrew switched on the TV to watch the local news which was running footage from Chesterfield, especially down Chatsworth Road. It was weird seeing the streets I knew well featured in the news, especially as I had seen some of the flooded areas first-hand. It wasn't just Chesterfield that featured, as many places across the country were experiencing similar issues.

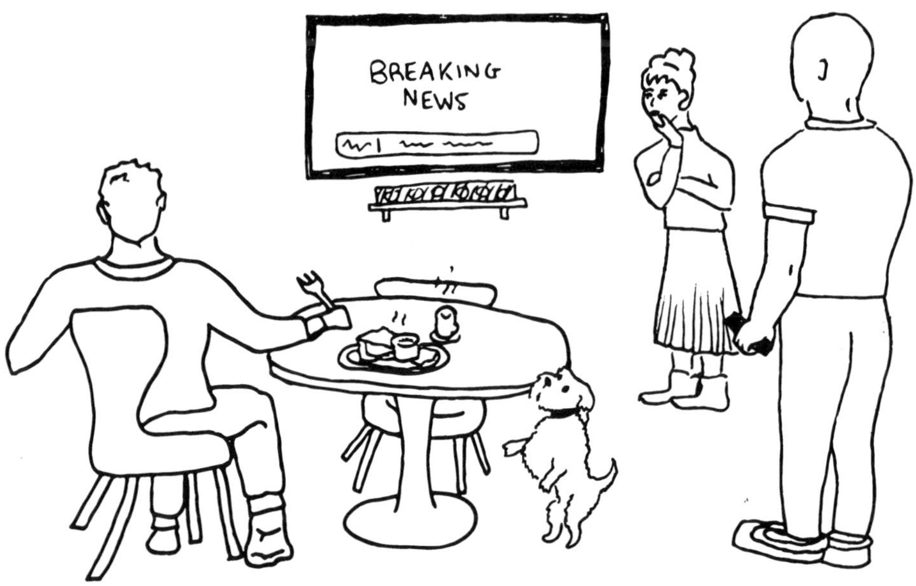

THE AFTER MATH

News Reporting

Storm Babet hit the UK between the 18 and 21 October 2023. The Met Office issued ninety flood warnings, with the storm causing severe flooding in Chesterfield on Friday, 20 October.

Babet was baptised on 16 October 2023, just a couple of days before it was due to hit the UK. Named storms are a relatively new concept in the UK, with the first being in 2015. Doing so signifies there will be medium to high impact to a region and ensures consistent reporting across the country.

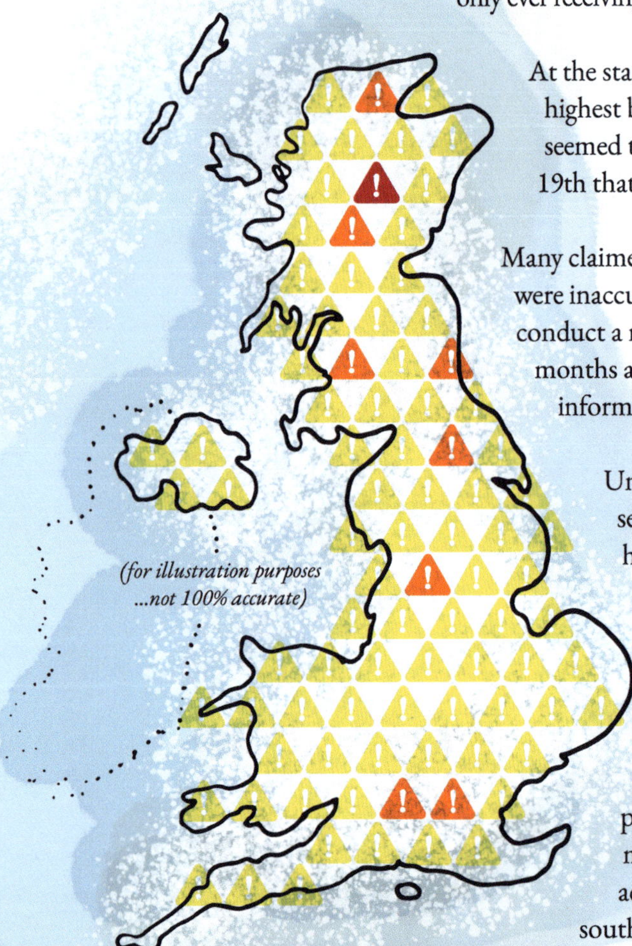

Much of the initial reporting during Storm Babet focused on Scotland and Northern Ireland, both of which saw the worst winds and rainfall. Initially, there wasn't much mention of the Midlands or the south east, with Suffolk and Norfolk only ever receiving a yellow weather warning. And yet both flooded badly.

At the start there weren't many weather warnings in place, with the highest being a yellow. In the run-up to the storm the warnings seemed to increase both in number and severity. It was only on the 19th that a rare red warning was issued for Scotland.

Many claimed that the forecasts and warnings about Storm Babet were inaccurate, which resulted in the Met Office saying they would conduct a review of their forecasting and warning system. Nine months after Babet, I have been unable to find any changes or any information from this 'review'.

Unfortunately, Storm Babet claimed the lives of at least seven people. It was miraculous that the number wasn't higher given the devastation it caused. Having advance warning clearly helped. It's all too easy to criticise and I wonder what would have happened if we'd had no warning at all?

I am not a meteorologist, but thanks to a report by Mike Kendon at the Met Office we know that a high pressure area over Scandinavia blocked Storm Babet from moving west to east, which is how storms usually move across the UK. This barrier meant that the storm moved south to north, allowing it to gain additional moisture from the Bay of Biscay. It then 'sat' on the UK for a prolonged period of time. Many long-running weather stations in England recorded their wettest October day. Which was true for the 139-year-old Sheffield station.

In layman's terms, Babet behaved differently to usual storms so it was more difficult to predict. This is why the warnings weren't as good as they perhaps could have been. The UK has a complex weather system, which makes trying to predict normal weather challenging. British weather is still a running joke across the country and I think the inaccurate weather reporting plays a large role. So I can see how something out of the ordinary can be even more difficult to get right.

Most people in the UK are probably also not aware that Portugal, Denmark, Norway and Germany also directly encountered Babet. I can't recall any of these countries mentioned in any form of reporting at the time.

Stories from these countries are well worth looking into if you find this interesting.

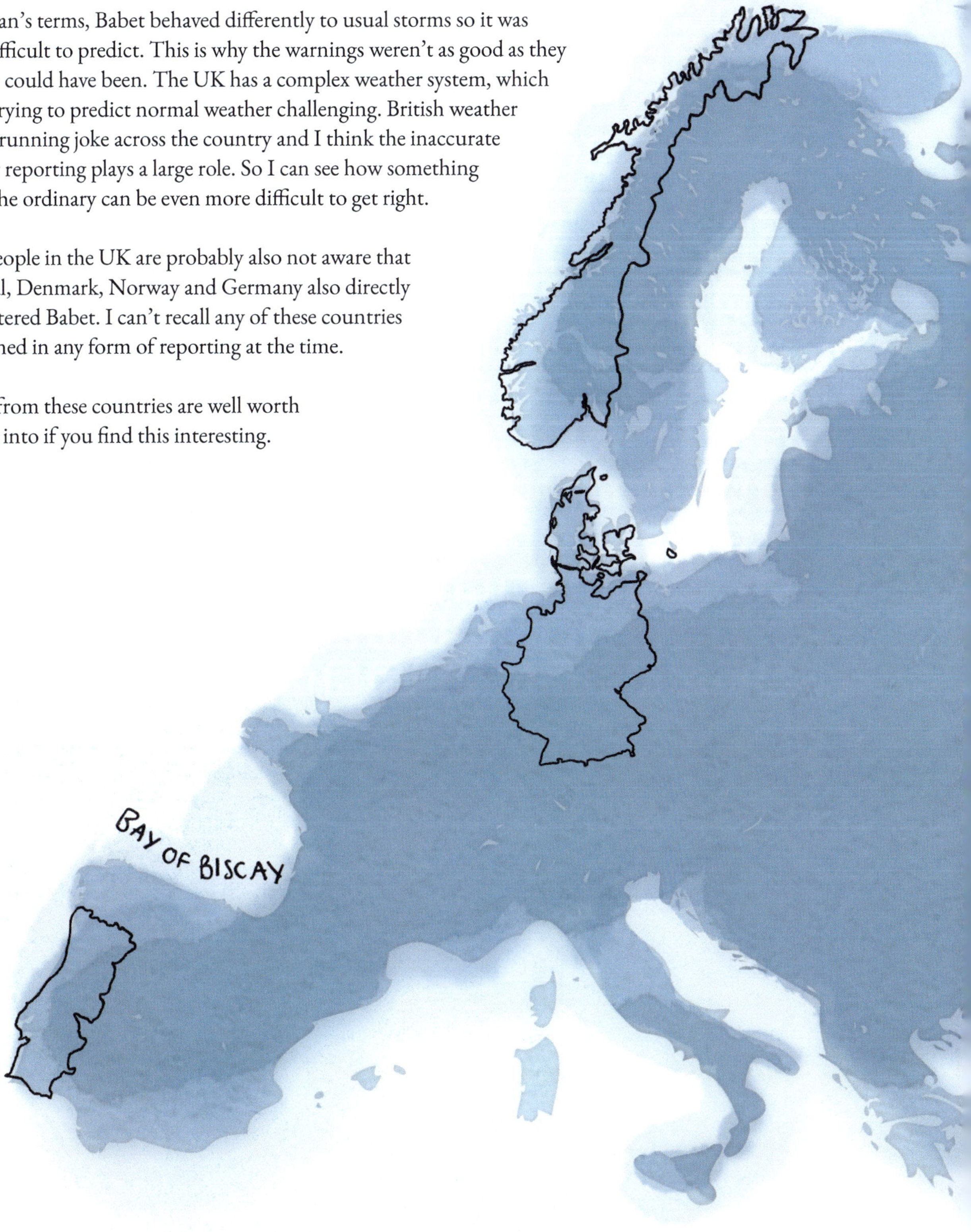

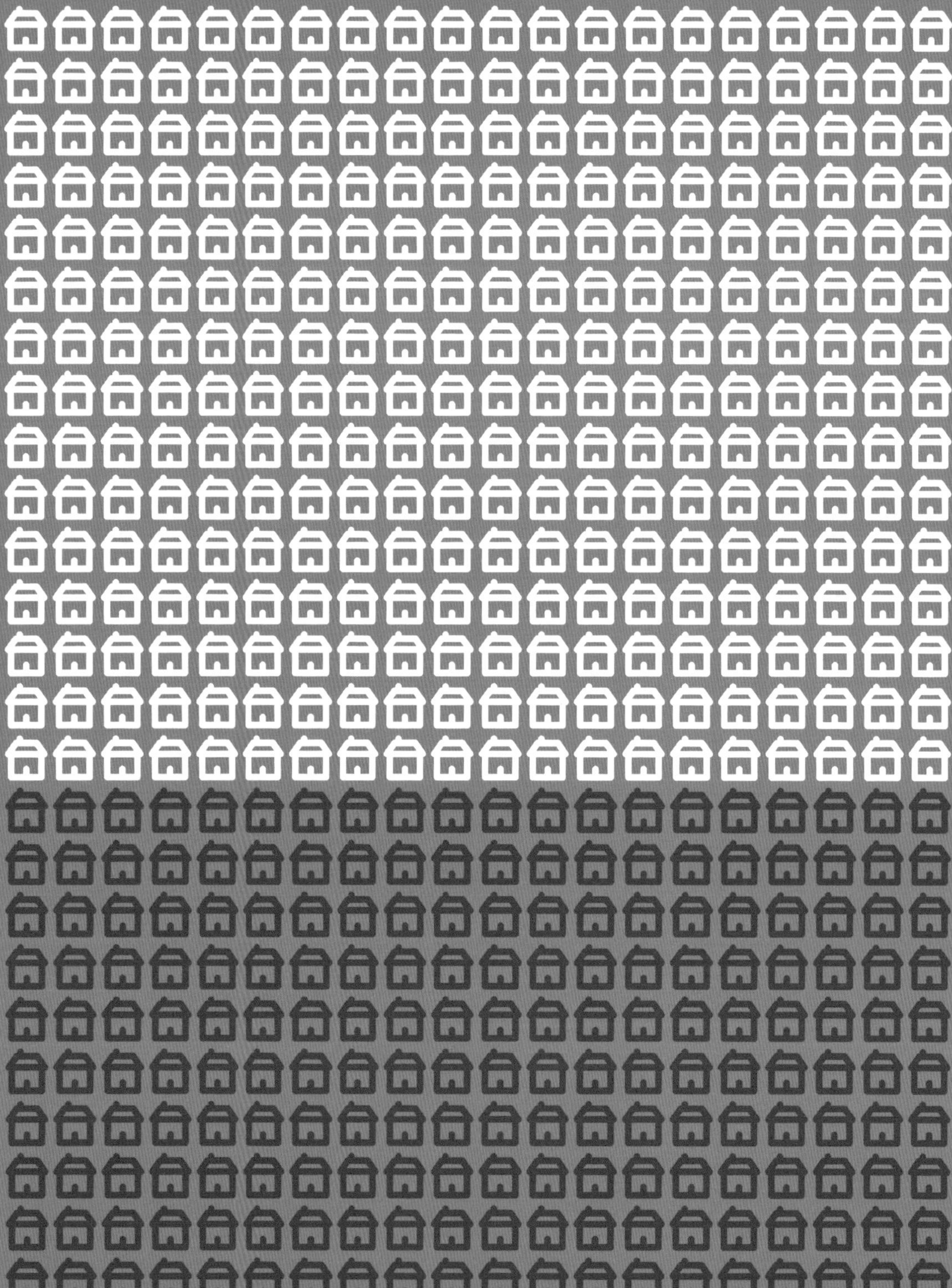

Over **1,000** homes were flooded in England. More than **400** were in Chesterfield.

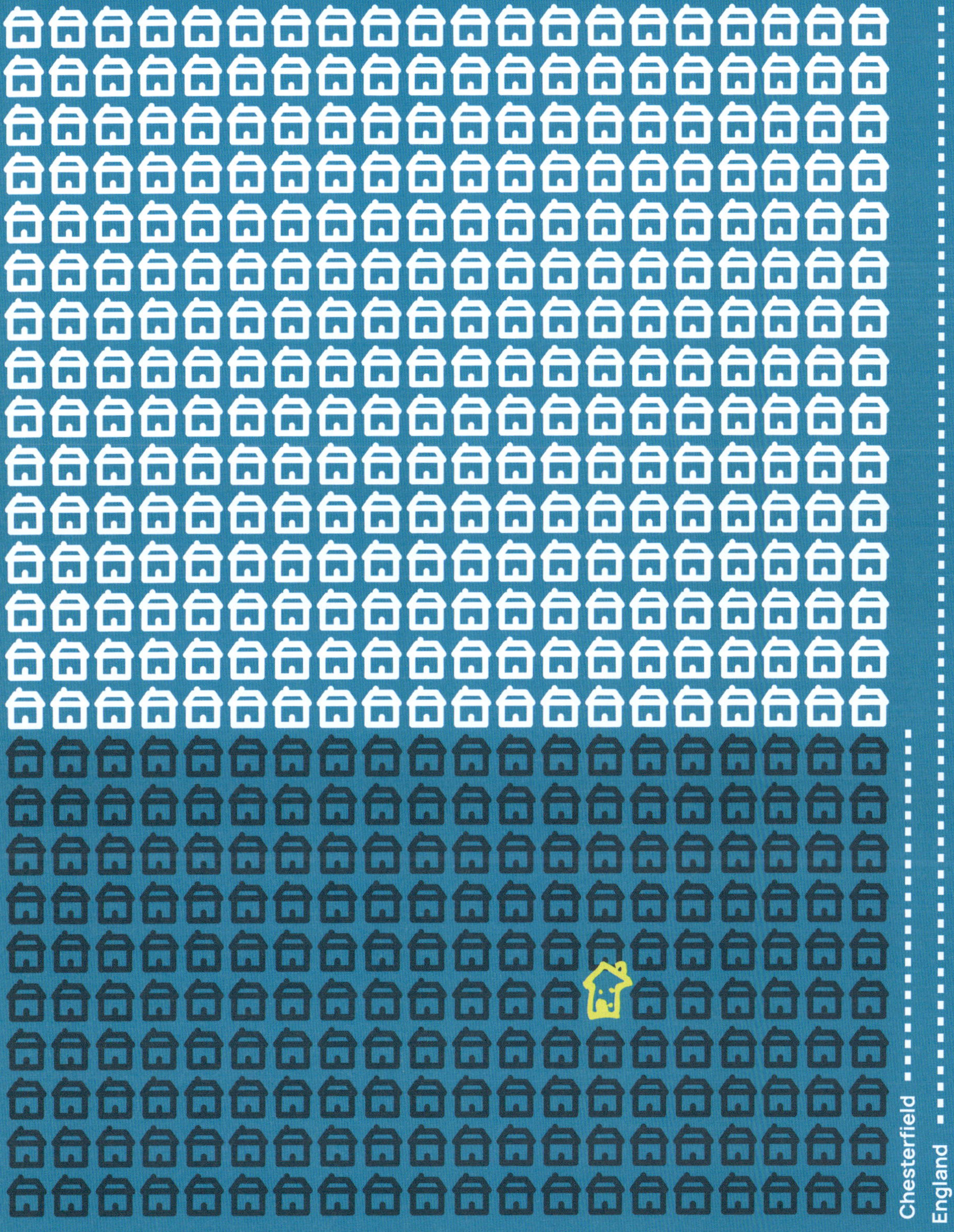

Oh, look! That's my house!

Following the news report, we played some vinyl records, with both Andrew and I messaging and contacting people to give updates and check in. During this time, I messaged various family members who had obviously seen the news and were concerned. Andrew discovered that John had made it back to his house safely.

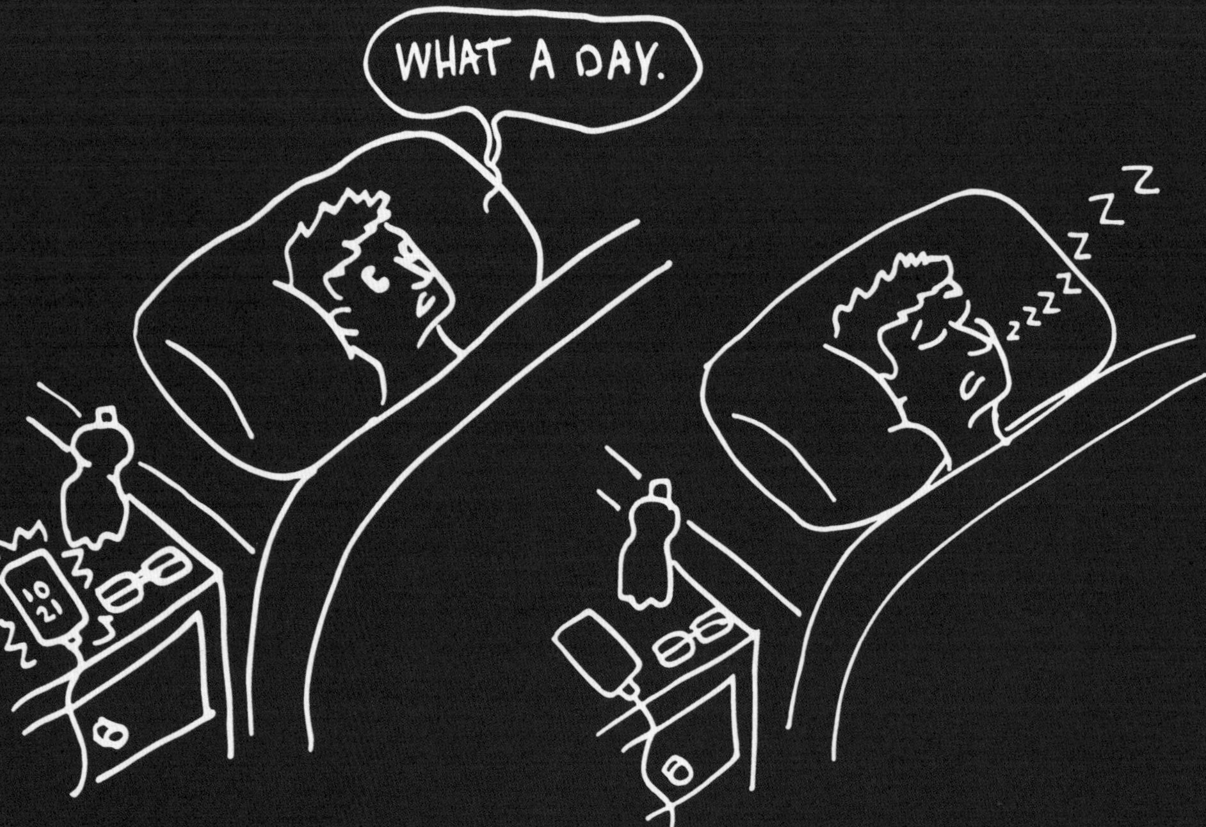

I messaged my landlord at around 9.00pm letting him know the situation and sharing the photos I had taken earlier in the day. He was very optimistic about the state of the flat; however, given what I had seen throughout the day, I was less so.

Calling it a night, I ventured to the guest room. Looking back, I remember how easy it was to get to sleep, easier than normal if I'm honest. I think at this stage I was happy to be dry and warm. Priorities shift in these circumstances and all the trivial worries and concerns don't matter. As far as I was concerned, I'd made it, having overcome the trials and tribulations of the day.

The Next Morning

For those whose houses were at a higher elevation this is practically the end of the story. Inconvenienced on the way home from work, having to wait in queues and getting tea later than usual. For those whose properties were flooded, it was just the beginning. While the damage occurred in a day, the restoration lasted for months.

Early the next morning, I had coffee with Andrew before setting off to work. Although it was Saturday, when the factory is normally shut, there was some concern this could also have been flooded. We thought it best to check, plus I'd be able to pick up my car. So, we borrowed Christina's car and drove in the direction of the factory. It was weird how the water that had flooded the streets was simply gone, leaving sheer devastation in its wake.

To get to work from Andrew's house, we had to drive past my flat. Andrew drove down Hady Hill and onto Camlough Walk, stopping outside the communal entrance to the flats where I lived, to see if I would be able to get in with my car. The first thing I noticed was the blanket of silt, dirt and sludge covering the ground. The second was the damage to the road surface itself with a lot of new potholes. It was definitely possible to access via car, though.

The communal entrance was propped open and had a clearly visible waterline on the wall. 'Do you want to take a look?' Andrew asked.

I stared out of the window at the entrance to my flat. 'No, let's go to work first,' I said. 'Whatever is waiting for me behind that door isn't going anywhere.' Plus, with so much sludge and dirt coating everything, it wasn't worth getting covered in it just yet.

We left Camlough Walk and drove towards work. The bottom of Hady Hill was fairly dry, apart from a coating of sludge. We noticed an abandoned saloon car under the bridge next to the Riverside pub. It occurred to us that this had been there yesterday; however, due to the height of the water level, it had been completely submerged so we couldn't see it. Andrew, along with everyone else, had to drive around it to get past. My commute to work is usually less than a ten-minute drive, but today it took significantly longer.

It was carnage, dodging and weaving around cars that had been abandoned in seemingly random places at almost every junction. Couple that with the layer of sludge on the roads and countless potholes and debris. Driving wasn't the safest. Andrew and I didn't really talk much during that journey; we were both too busy taking in the damage surrounding us.

We made it to work without incident and found that the car park was unaffected, which meant everyone who had left their cars overnight could sigh in relief. Naturally, this meant that my car was okay, phew!

Andrew and I entered the factory and had a look around to check that there were no internal issues or roof leakage. Amazingly, it was all fine, which was great news. With such a large number of people employed at our site, many people's livelihoods were at stake.

Andrew then gave me a key to the office and set me up with a code for the alarm system. This was immensely useful. Due to my role I have a desk there with a computer that I use every day. I had tools and resources to assist me in the battles to come.

With that, we parted ways, and I set off for my flat.

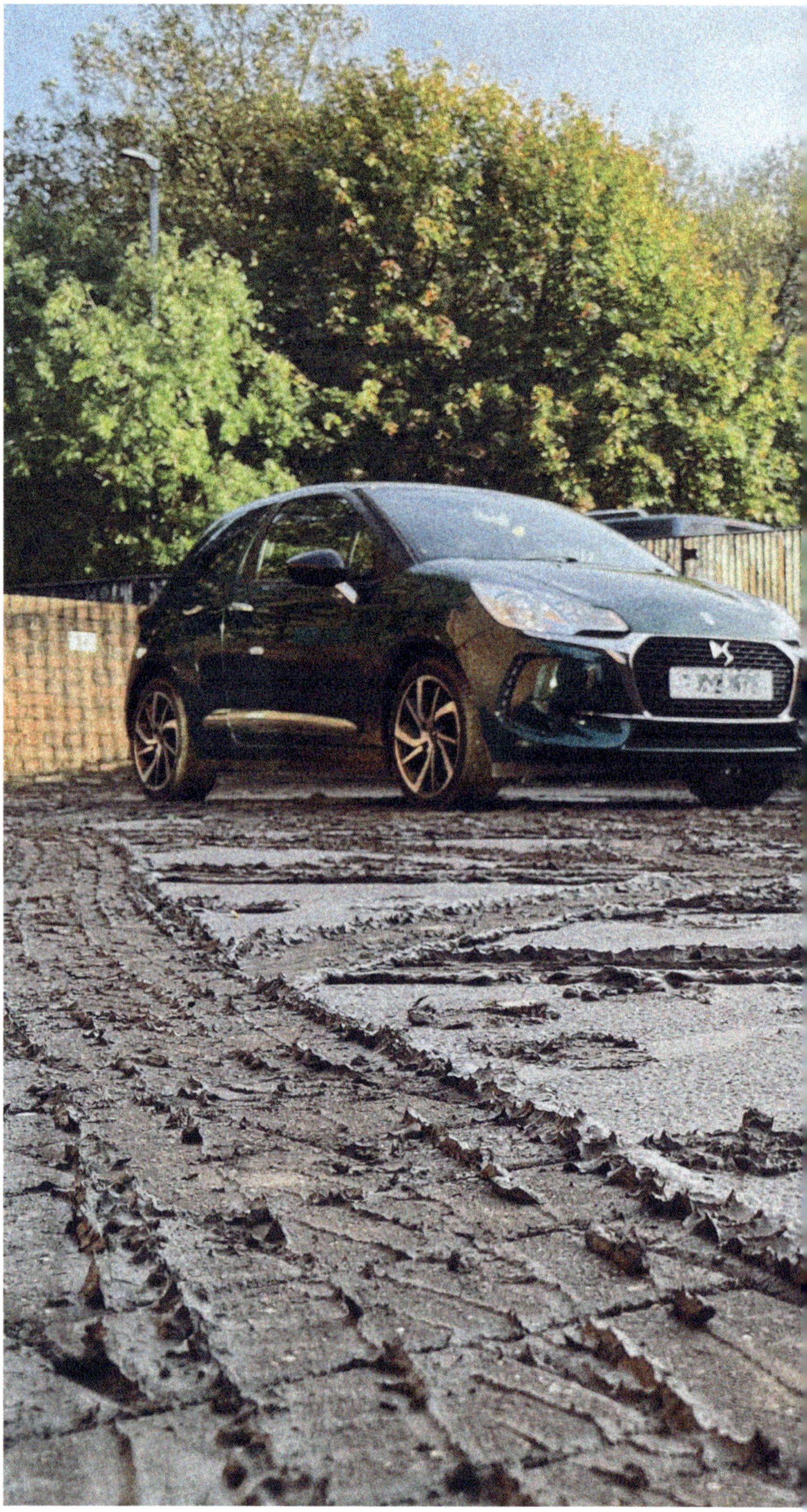

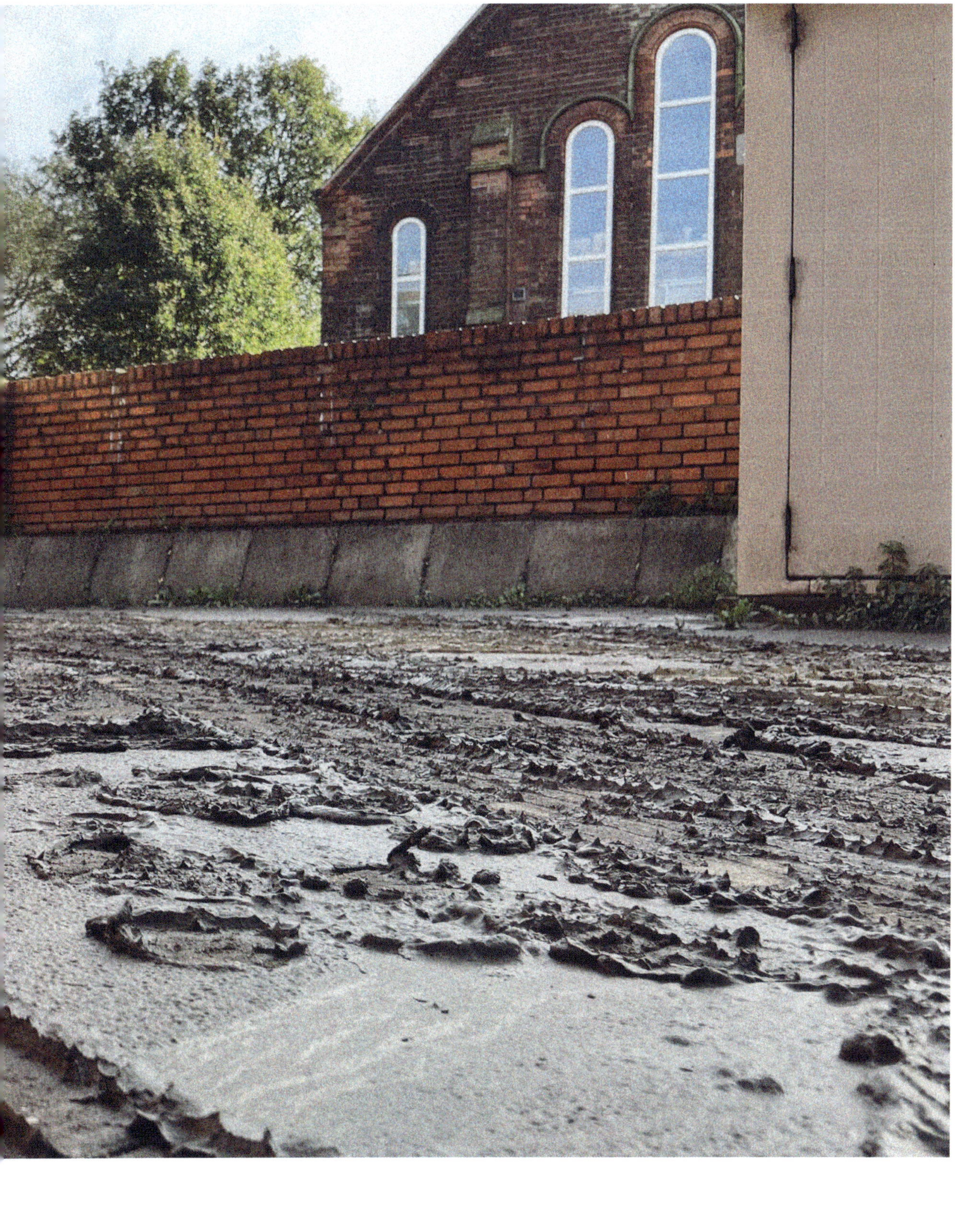

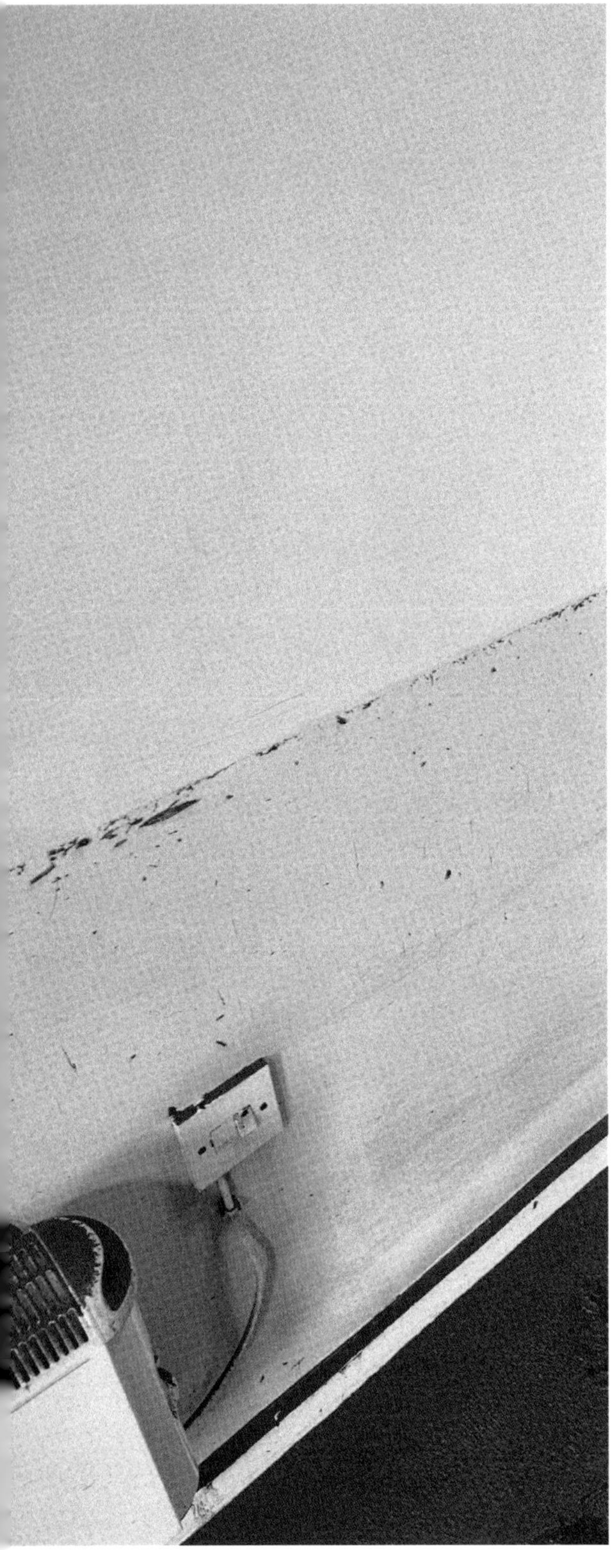

My Flat

The drive there was difficult. The eastbound lane at the bottom of Hady Hill had been closed. Luckily, this was reopened later that day when the abandoned cars were cleared. It did mean I had to take a half-hour detour with a lot of other people in the same situation.

This improvised route resulted in me driving under the bridge at Crow Lane, which still had the abandoned car under it from yesterday. Again though there was no water in sight, I vividly remember that the world seemed to 'steam' wherever the sun hit that morning, especially in this area. I really wish I had taken a photo as you could see the water vapour entering the atmosphere as if all of Chesterfield was on the washing line trying to dry. However, I was too focused on getting back to my flat.

It had taken me twenty-one hours to finally arrive home. I guess you could say that was my true commute time. You can see from the photos that a layer of silt and sludge coated the ground everywhere. I parked up in my designated spot, my car's tyres being the first to cut through this sludge to expose the brick road below. I changed into my wellies straight away and walked over to the main entrance. I took photos as I walked in, so you are experiencing the devastation first-hand with me.

The first thing that struck me was the waterline; it was high, I would guess about four feet from the ground. I took a breath, unlocked the door and entered my flat. Well, I tried to enter but the door wouldn't budge. Though unexpected, I reasoned that it must just be the carpet expanding. I gave the door a few hard shoves to open it. To my surprise, there was a pile of my belongings that had also prevented the door from opening. This was strange, as I hadn't left any of them by the door before leaving.

The next thing I found odd was that everything had moved; my bed, sofas and various other items had

Commute times: 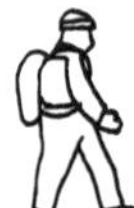 *Andrew: 4hr 25m* 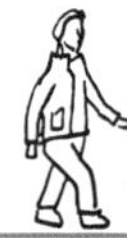 *John: 6hr 30m* obviously floated around. It sounds obvious but it wasn't something I had anticipated. I had expected everything to be where I left it – just wet.

Even more bizarre was that everything on my coffee table (which wasn't very high off the ground) was undamaged. So evidently the table had floated above the level of the water. It's funny to think of the heavy wooden coffee table floating in such a gentle and gradual way. Its surface being seemingly frozen in time, with the surrounding environment having dramatically changed. A full kitchen roll stood proudly on top, completely dry. My book and coffee mug were exactly as I had left them the day previously. In fact, I still have that same book now.

It was such a surreal experience. I was at a loss for what to do next and overwhelmed by the magnitude of the damage. I found myself randomly wandering around exploring this new environment, taking photos as I did so. For the first quarter of an hour, I didn't touch or move anything, as I tried to process that it was actually real.

Homes hold our memories, provide a retreat to return to and a haven for when we are sick. They are incredibly personal spaces, taking on the character of those who live within them. We all make some effort to mould them to our liking. It felt like part of myself was lost.

I sent photos to my landlord and, needless to say, he was shocked. He made the decision to drive over and see the damage first-hand. I made sure to warn him about the current state of Chesterfield's roads and that some road closures were still in effect.

Condensation had already built up on the inside of the windows, and the air in the room felt muggy and thick. Not wanting to get ill, I opened all the windows. One fault of this flat was that all the windows faced east, so it was dingy most of the time. An upside was that the windows were large and could be opened wide, which helped to provide good ventilation.

I tried the lights, and fortunately they worked. Knowing the water had risen above the plug sockets, I didn't even think about using them. Instead, I went to the fuse box and ensured everything other than lighting was switched off. As it happened, most, if not all, had already tripped out.

I then removed all plugs from the walls. The first thing I unplugged was an air purifier in my bedroom. Water gushed out of the wall socket. Not just a little bit either. It made a notable puddle on the floor. I have never seen anything like it. With every plug I removed, a new puddle formed.

Interestingly, water can become trapped in strange ways; it might be from a chair you move or a washing-up bowl or a glass on a low shelf. Lots of these tricky places catch you off-guard and, sometimes, I would open things only for water to gush out.

The worst two instances of this were my washing machine and dishwasher. Both were completely full of water and could only be emptied by opening the doors. This was bizarre to me. They were closed and by their very nature should be water tight, right? How then did both get full of water that did not then leak out? The most likely explanation I could come up with was the drains backing up, and in the process making both appliances flood internally. Some appliances have one-way valves which could prevent this; I'm not sure if these did.

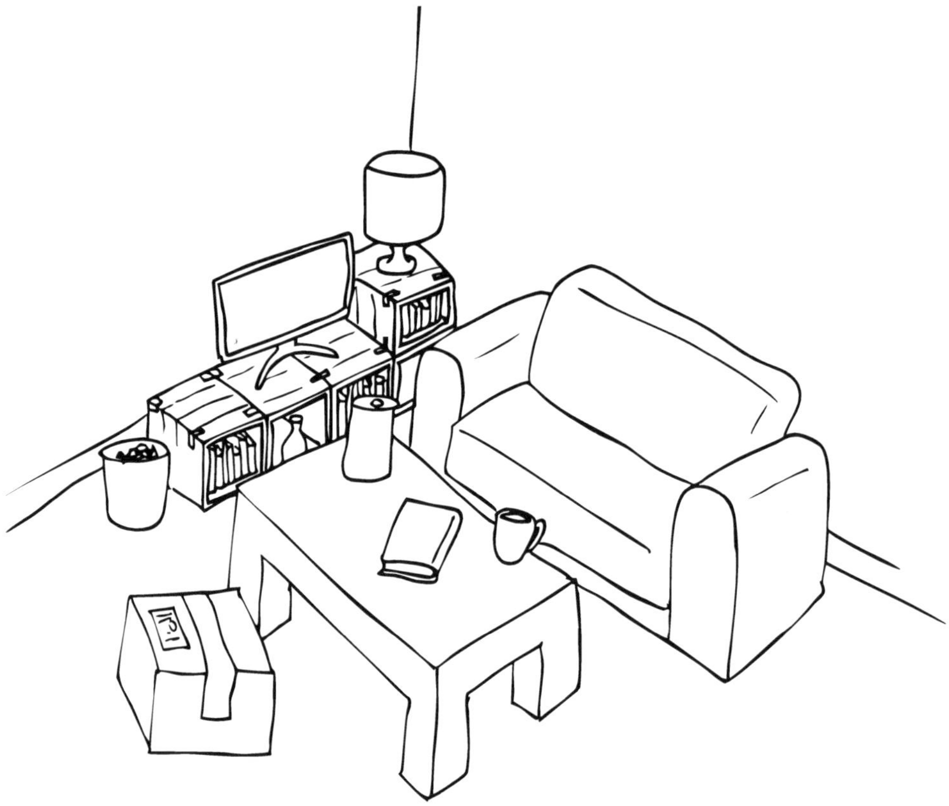

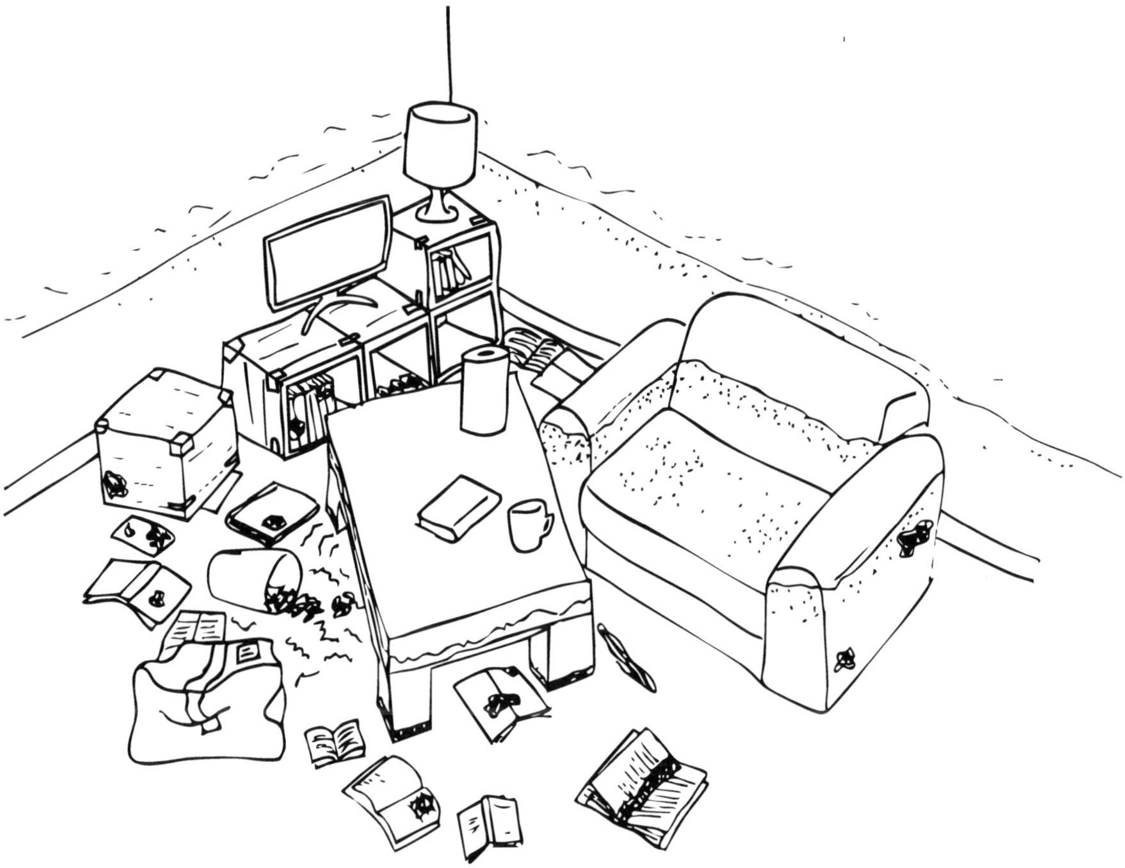

To start with, I cleared out the hallways and made pathways into all the rooms. Because everything was arbitrarily scattered on the floor, I was constantly stepping over things to get anywhere. At first, this just involved throwing things into corners or out of the way so that I had a clear path around. Trying to be proactive, I attempted to mop the floor in my kitchen, though I quickly realised it was a pointless exercise at this early stage of the clean-up operation.

Instead, I decided to clear up slightly by throwing some rubbish into bin liners. The flooding had resulted in both my general waste and recycling floating around the room. So, I took care of this first before anything else. I entered my bedroom and checked my mattress. I initially thought it might be salvageable but soon realised that it was drenched. The floor was also incredibly uneven because it had absorbed so much water.

As you can probably tell, I couldn't focus, and my thoughts jumped all over the place as I wondered what I should do next. I went from one thing to the next, bouncing back and forth between half doing one thing and half doing something else.

After some time had passed, I realised the first problem was where I would stay? The flat was uninhabitable in its current state, and it would take some time to dry out and deal with the water damage. My family all live in Hull, so it was possible for me to go there, but then I would face an hour and a half commute to and from Chesterfield (or longer, due to current roadworks on the M62 Ouse Bridge).

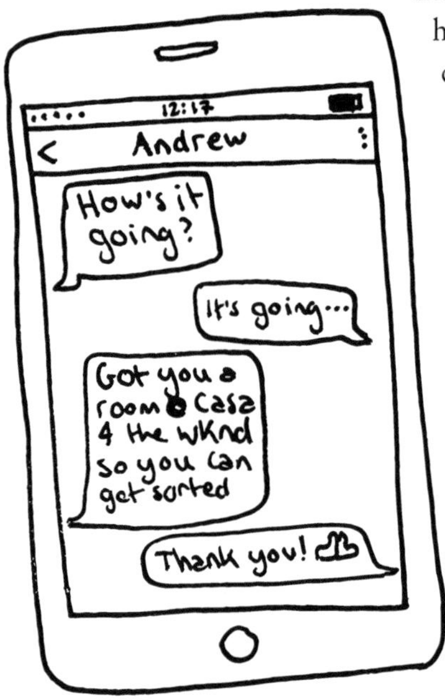

It was around this time that Andrew messaged me asking about the state of things. After reading my synopsis of the situation, he rang me to tell me that he'd booked me into a local hotel called the Casa over the weekend, to allow me time to get sorted. This ended up being extended for a week, for which I am very thankful as it allowed me time and space to organise things.

This breakthrough allowed me to collect my thoughts. At the very least I had somewhere to stay and, knowing I could use my work office to get things done, enabled me to think more clearly. It also removed the pressure of having to do everything, and it didn't matter if the mattress was wet or the hallway was muddy.

That was when my landlord knocked on the door.

I think anyone who rents property will have experienced the dreaded landlord inspection. This one was a little different though. I'd never met him in person before this point, as the estate agent had dealt with advertising and signing of the contracts. However, the landlord managed to make it into Chesterfield to visit the flat that day, and I recall how shocked he was when he entered.

In retrospect, I had already had time to process the scene; however, this was all fresh to him and far worse than he was expecting. During his visit, he had a discussion with the owners of the upstairs flats about building insurance. I must admit my only thought at that time was: ***Go home so that I can start sorting things out!***

However, before I could do anything further, the decision was made not to try to clean up as the damage was too severe. Even at this early stage, you could feel that the whole floor had warped dramatically. It almost made you seasick walking around on the wavy floor! Knowing that it wasn't my job to put it all right was a big relief, too.

To his credit, the landlord released me from my rental contract without any hesitation. So I am grateful to him, as it was one less thing to worry about. We said goodbye and I shut the door to the flat, leaving me on my own to figure things out.

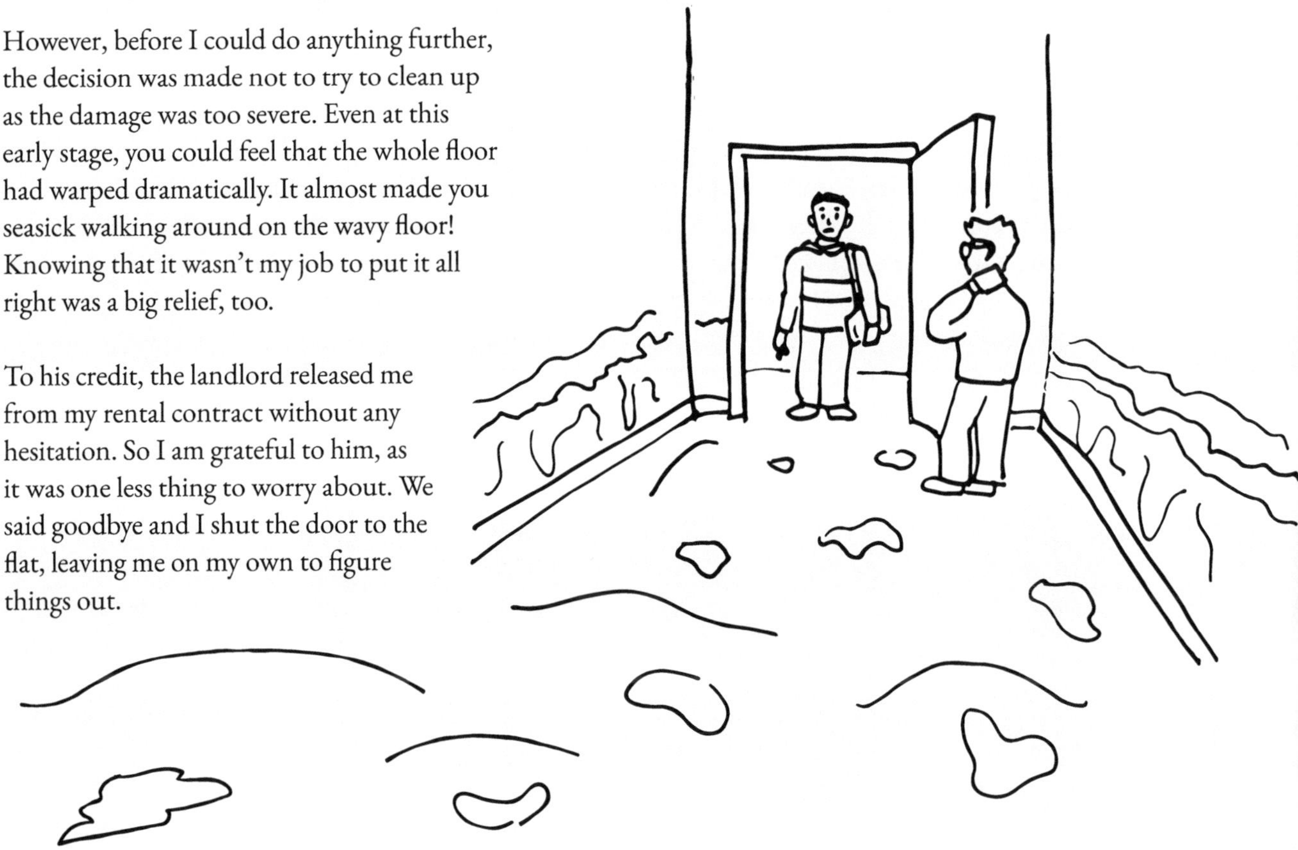

Looking around, I realised practically everything I owned had been destroyed.

I thought back to that fateful day at the estate agents when I signed the contract for the flat. I sat in a chair opposite the estate agent as she tapped on a keyboard. After a few minutes, I was given a price for the contents insurance they brokered, but I didn't know enough about the market so decided against it. I planned to research further before committing to anything. The estate agent then offered to send the quote in an email so that I could apply later if I changed my mind. With that, I was handed the keys to my new flat and headed over straight away.

I had been so excited to call this place my own and not be sharing with anyone. I made sure to set up my council tax, electric, water and internet. Then I compared prices on contents insurance. Discovering that the price I had been given by the estate agent was competitive, I asked them if it covered flooding with the flat being next to a river. They confirmed that it did, and I decided to take them up on this offer. I didn't know then how glad I would be later.

Returning to my now flooded abode, I sat on my coffee table, as the couches were soaked through, and I rang up my insurance company. I wanted to check that I was definitely covered for flood damage. I had this paranoia that I wouldn't be. On that phone call they confirmed that I was. It was such a relief. Of all the decisions I've made in my life, getting contents insurance with flood protection was one of the best. The company informed me that my claim had been logged and they would get back to me about what to do next. Due to the sheer number of claims at this time, they warned me that this could take a bit longer than usual. However, they would contact me later that day or the day after.

I was much calmer after this as I had somewhere to stay and knew that I had financial cover for my personal belongings. Now came the battle to restore order to my life. The only way out of this mess was through it. With this a new sense of clarity took over.

If I was going to be at the flat clearing things for some time, I'd require a functioning bathroom. The residents were all informed that the plumbing was safe and could be used. I, therefore, set about cleaning the bath and sink so that I had somewhere to wash things and could use the toilet. I may not have hot water anymore, but I still had cold running water, and this made things much easier. The process of cleaning basically involved turning on the shower and rinsing the entire room, and then dousing everything in a healthy coating of bleach. I then mopped up the dirty water as best I could.

My toolbox was full of water and gunk so I put it into my bath and started washing everything out to try and save what I could. Unfortunately, I still had to throw away some things. I left the surviving items in the bath to dry.

I then set about tidying up my living room by putting anything that was completely wrecked into bin bags. It turned out that this was a complete waste of time, as I will discuss later.

I was thankful it was a Saturday, as it meant I didn't have to worry about work. By now it was well past lunchtime and I hadn't eaten yet. I picked up a burger and headed to the office.

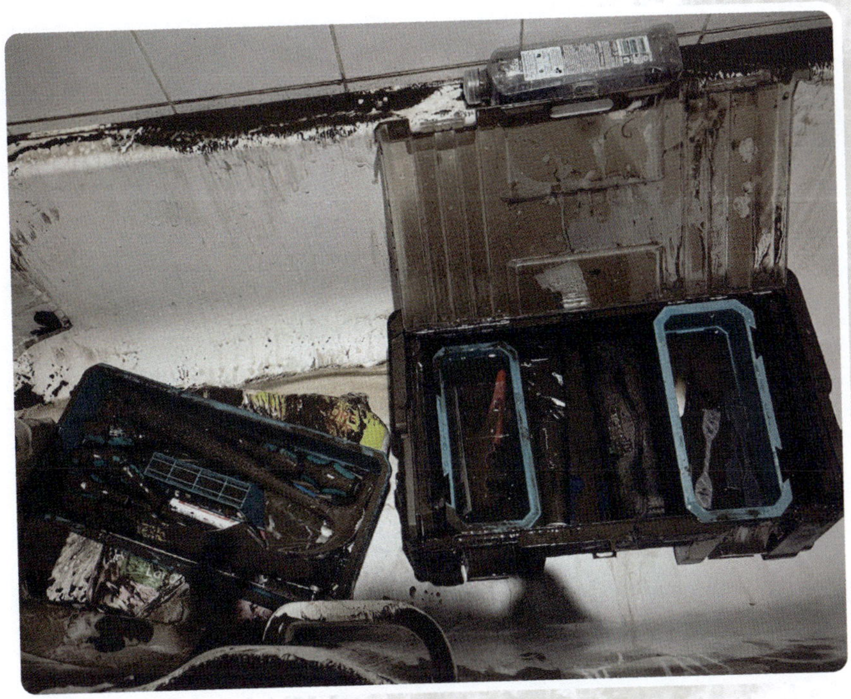

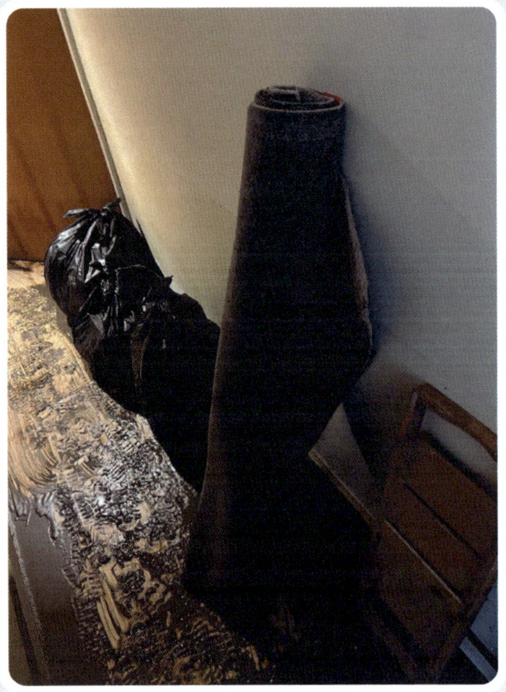
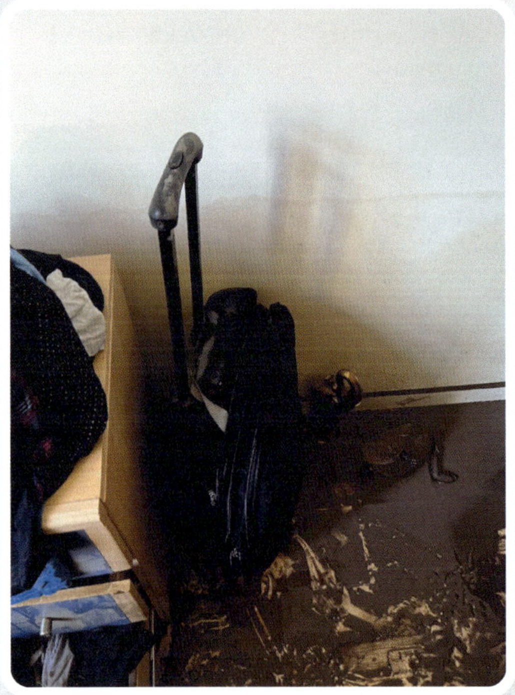
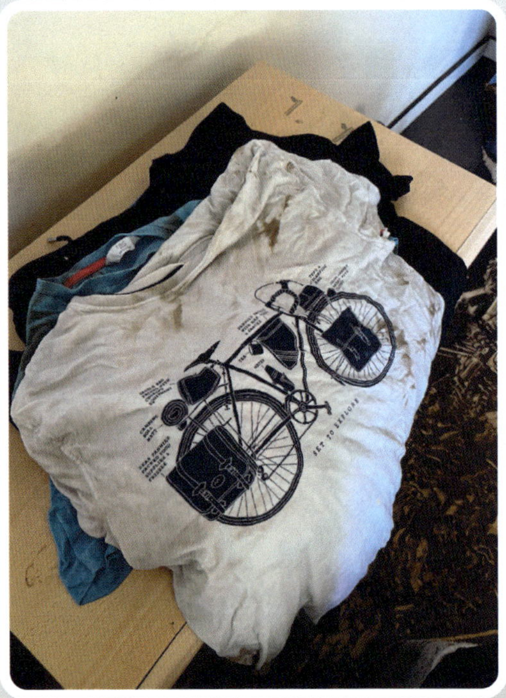
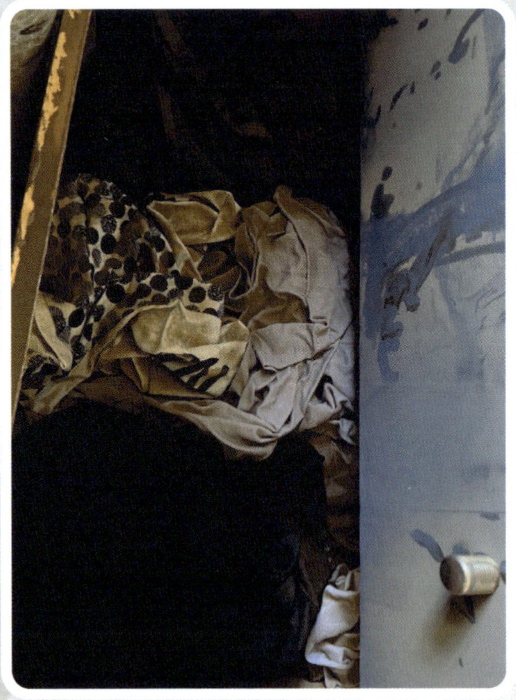

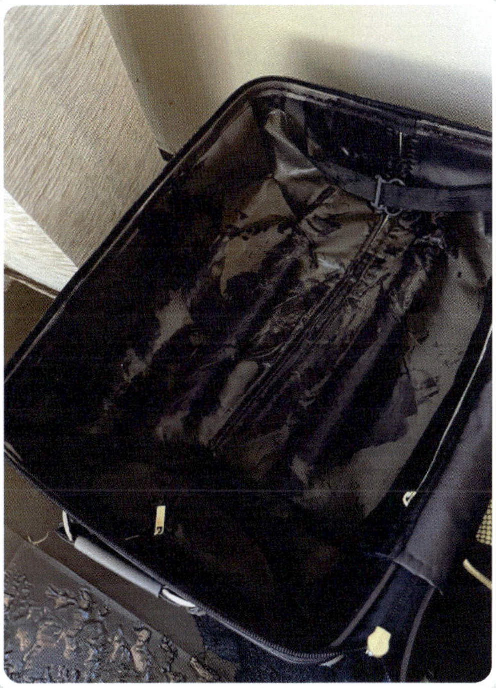

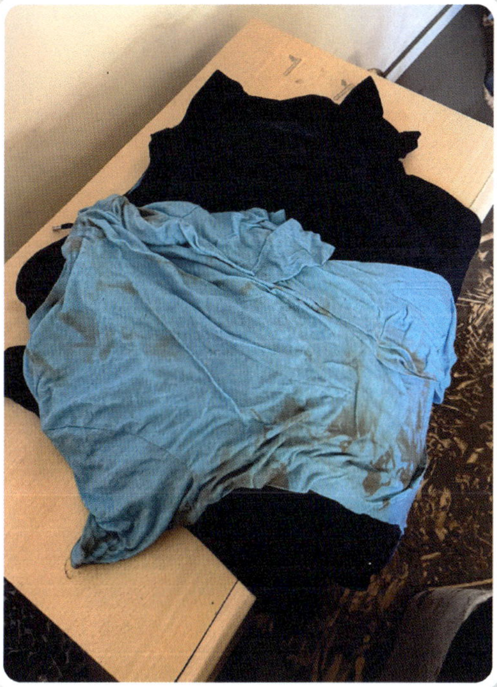

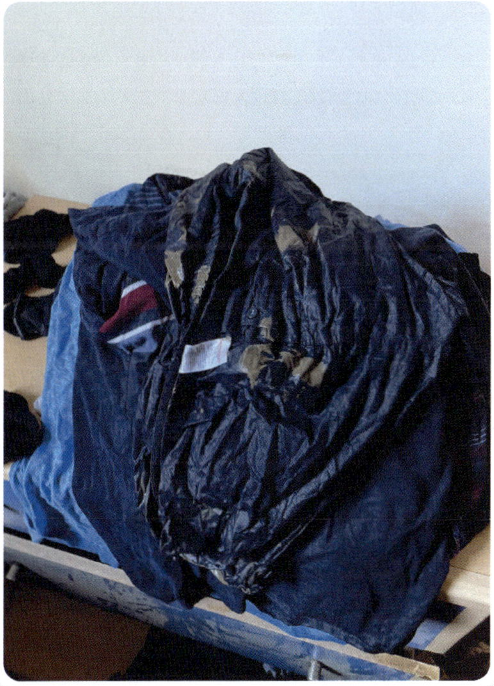

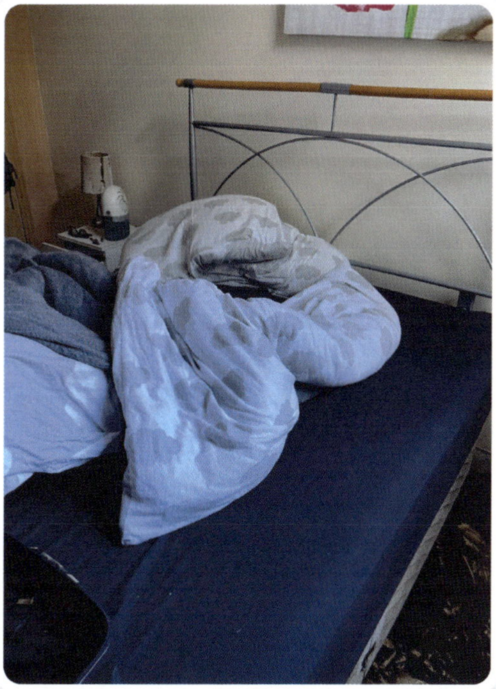

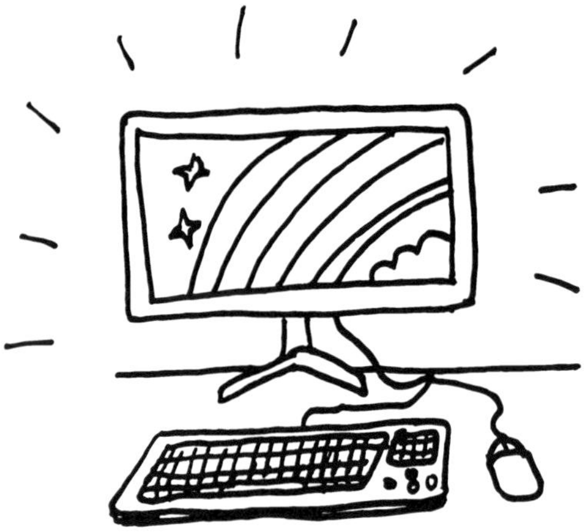

My place of work became a kind of sanctuary, away from the chaos of my flat, and still a normal and familiar environment. I also had a desk with a computer, which meant I could easily access the internet and send/receive important files relating to my current situation. I cannot stress enough how having this working space available increased the speed at which I was able to do things. There is only so much you can do on a phone screen. It also gave me a place to sit down, as all my soft furnishings were soaked still and completely unusable.

It was only then I realised I no longer had a charger; luckily I have one at work, so I borrowed that for the time being. I used my phone heavily during this time, and as I was expecting calls from the insurance company, I really needed it to be working.

Having eaten, I returned to my flat. I was going to need clothes, so I went into my bedroom to check what had survived. Typically, most of my clothes were in the laundry basket on the floor. As the water level was so high, it had also taken out everything in my chest of drawers. When I opened the drawers, there were pools of water in them.

The long and short of this was that I had no trousers, shirts, or underwear. Great!

Even just moving around was risky as the sludge on the floor was very slippy. I didn't even have a suitcase anymore as that, too, was totally drenched. Fortunately, I had an overnight bag on top of my wardrobe that was clean.

Whatever I could save I packed into my car. To be honest, it wasn't much as I barely filled the boot of my small car. I think it mainly amounted to the items I had taken with me to work the day previously, an overnight bag and that was it.

Those of us who had been flooded on the ground floor all seemed to exchange this look and a nod as if to say: I know it's bad but keep going. I experienced this same phenomenon with other people on the street; people whose homes had also been flooded. Usually no words were exchanged, but if they were it was always a subdued greeting. In comparison, the people from higher floors tended to be more chatty. I appreciated their good intentions, but it was something I found annoying as I had a lot to do. Standing around moaning about the situation isn't something I enjoy or find useful.

I stayed at the flat sorting through things until it was completely dark outside and I decided to call it a night. It was, by this time, around 10.30pm.

Hotel Visit

I drove carefully through the streets to get to the hotel; some roads were still closed and there was debris and crud everywhere. With everyone forced onto the same back lanes and makeshift workaround routes, congestion was heavy. I noticed car boot windows packed to the brim with personal possessions and realised these people were in a similar situation to myself. We were all fleeing from the inhospitable housing that, just the day before, had been home.

To put this in perspective, the Casa is a four-star hotel, and I believe it to be the most upmarket hotel in Chesterfield. And on that day a sweaty man walked into reception covered in flood grunge, looking somewhat the worse for wear. At the time, though, I didn't care. I walked through the posh foyer and up to the reception desk clutching the few possessions that were undamaged by the flood. On talking to the receptionist, I discovered that quite a few people had already checked in due to the floods. The staff were always very nice while conversing with these displaced individuals.

Arriving at my room on the second floor, room 214, I opened the door for the first time. The privilege of having this room was not lost on me as it was stunning to say the least. Throwing my things on the floor next to the bed, I wasted no time in checking out the luxurious bathroom. I went to take a shower and realised I didn't have any toiletries. The hotel provided a few basics, and for now this had to do. I changed into the only set of dry, clean clothes I owned. Those I had worn to work the previous day that Christina had laundered for me.

I didn't even have a toothbrush. Thinking about it, neither did I have any shaving supplies, deodorant or aftershave. After my shower, I headed over the road to the nearby supermarket. Fortunately, it was open until midnight so I was able to grab some essentials. While there I realised I should purchase more clothes, but I was so tired by this point I decided it could wait until the next day. I returned to my hotel room with my emergency purchases.

By now it was late and I was extremely hungry. I should have bought something while I was out but had completely forgotten. Therefore, I decided to order room service for the first time in my life. By that hour the menu was limited so I settled for a simple pizza.

After finishing my meal, I placed the tray outside and brushed my teeth. I climbed into bed and set an alarm for early next morning. My company was kind enough to pay for breakfast as part of the room, which I enjoyed every day I stayed there. Usually, I went for a full English, which was empowering to say the least.

The next day being a Sunday, I had plenty of time to begin sorting things out. After breakfast I changed out of my 'clean' clothes and into what I dubbed my 'dirty' set for going to my flat. While driving, I noticed how much the roads had improved. There were no abandoned cars in the middle of lanes, and no debris either. All roads were open and seemingly safe to drive on. I will say that there was damage to the surface of the roads, with new potholes and cracks in the tarmac.

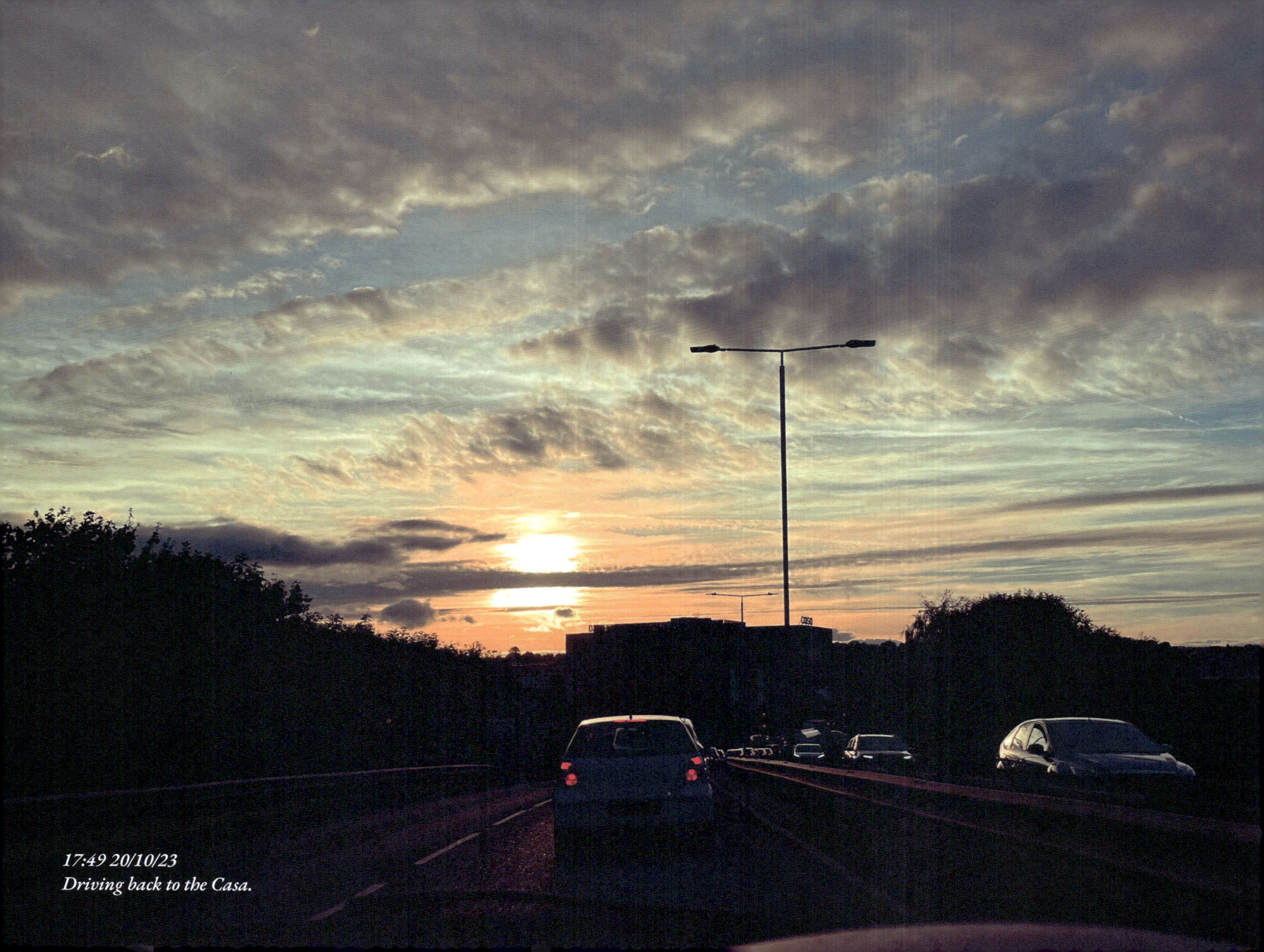

17:49 20/10/23
Driving back to the Casa.

I changed into my wellies upon arrival and headed straight into my flat. This time there was no lingering around looking at the damage. I had become somewhat accustomed to it. There was a nice warm glow in my flat that morning; the sun was still low in the sky and it felt like a brighter day than before. It was also the first day that the sun had really come out since the flooding. It illuminated the world in full colour again after spending the past few days in greyscale.

I had so many phone conversations with my insurance company and their contracted loss adjusters that I've lost track of what exactly happened when. The important thing was that I had a very clear sense of what the plan was moving forward. I had to create a long list of all the damaged items with accompanying photos and find a price and a link for them to share with the insurance company.

While doing this, I could put some of my damaged possessions in bin bags ready to be removed. My insurance company asked me to send them my most expensive belongings, so that they could see if anything could be repaired. This mainly consisted of technology items, which I piled on my coffee table.

This was slightly annoying as I ended up having to open all the bags of stuff I'd thrown away the previous day, take a photo of the items and then rebag them all. Soon there were five or six full bin bags at my door ready to be thrown away

All the flats shared a fenced-in communal bin area. The large commercial-sized bins had floated in the flood and blocked the main entrance to this area. With no other option, I initially had to leave the bin bags in my hallway.

While I was busy cleaning, Chesterfield Council had come to rectify this. They had also put lots of bins down the entire road and, on our side alone, there were probably five. On top of that, you could leave any larger items at the side of the road for them to come around and collect. As you might expect, these bins were soon full and the roadside piles grew quickly. However, I saw council vans come up and down the street multiple times per day to collect and take things away. I was impressed by how quickly this was in place and how well it seemed to work.

It remained busy for the first couple of days, with lots of activity, and the bins always seemed to be full. My main concern wasn't getting all the damaged items out of the flat, it was ensuring I documented everything for the insurance claim.

Around lunch time, I grabbed another takeaway and headed to work for a rest. While I was there, I received a message saying my package had been delivered. Argh! I had forgotten that I had recently been ordering healthy food from an online company. At first I cursed, thinking it was a waste of food and money, as the box had been dumped outside my flat on the muddy floor. I had nowhere to put any of this. Then I realised this was actually a blessing. I rushed back to my flat to pick up the package, removed the contents and put them in my boot, before going straight back to work.

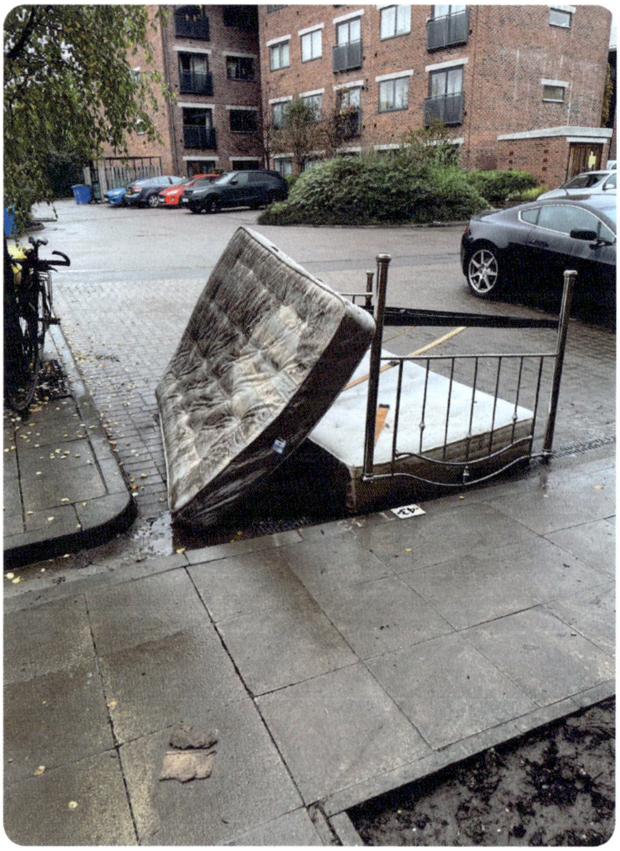

Fortunately, we have a few fridges so I took everything out and stored it at work. This would cover my lunch and dinner meals for a few days, and I didn't have to worry about living off takeaways constantly. Have you ever noticed that in films and TV shows no one ever has to deal with the logistics of preparing food and eating? For example, going out and purchasing food or stocking up the fridge. Spending ages thinking about what you want. Cursing when you're missing an ingredient or something has gone off. These practicalities never seem to come up in adventure stories. Well, I survived on a mixture of restaurant breakfasts and evening meals, takeaways and now the healthy food delivery. These meals just needed heating in a microwave for a few minutes. With my food safely stored, I returned to my flat.

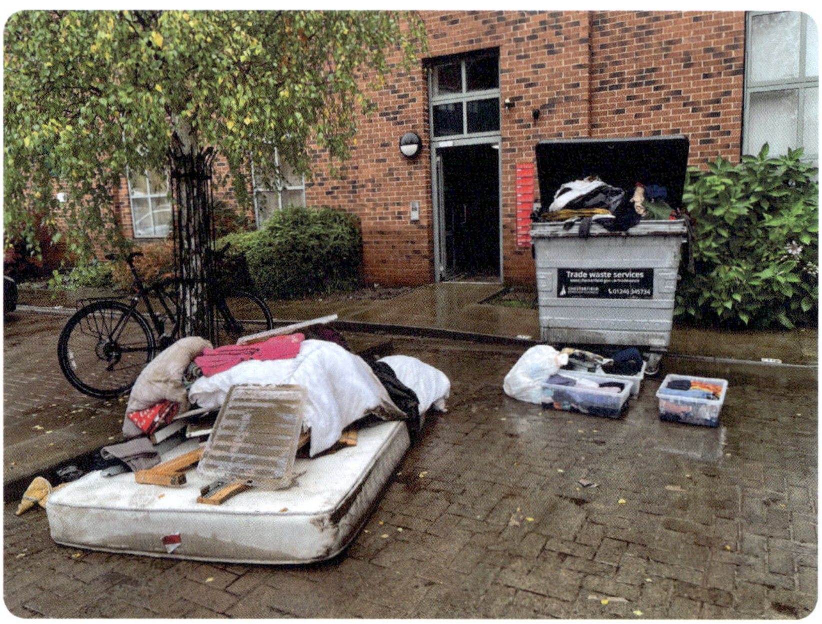

Story of The Upstairs Flat

When my key was half in the door, one of my upstairs neighbours, we'll call her 'Sarah', snuck up behind me on the staircase and asked how I was doing. *To be honest, I've just realised how comical it was that I kept incessantly locking the door each time I left. Let's face it, the damage was done!*

Naturally my response was the vague standard British 'yeah, fine thanks' and was not really an answer. If I'm being completely honest, I didn't want to talk. I was focused, no, fixated, on the task at hand. I wasn't going to be rude though, so I made small talk with Sarah about what was happening and how terrible it was. However, I did hear a rather interesting story about her experience that I didn't fully appreciate at the time.

Sarah and her husband, who we will call 'Bob', purchased an upstairs flat together a few years ago. Bob turned out to be the man my landlord had spent ages talking to about building insurance. I had hoped to use their first-hand account here; however, I didn't hear back after trying to contact them. As such, I have changed their names and will tell you their story myself.

To be honest, this was the first occasion I'd met either of them. It's odd how bad situations bring people together, isn't it? Thinking about it, I saw more of my neighbours during this time then I had in the eight months since I'd moved in.

Sarah told me how they had both been in the flat when the flooding began. By the time the water was an inch or two deep, people started to get worried. At first, Bob had been helping people to move their cars out of the way. Again, this was something I wish I'd clarified. I've assumed this to mean that he followed them in his car and, when they had parked at the top of Hady Hill, drove them back to Camlough Walk.

According to Sarah, the water seemed to increase slowly before all of a sudden rising rapidly. Most people who were living in these flats decided to evacuate and stay at a hotel for the night. She said they had walked to the hotel on Lordsmill Roundabout, which might have been possible at one point if the water level was lower. At 4.30pm, by the time Andrew, John and I arrived at the base of Hady Hill, there was no way anyone was getting through. The only way to make it to that hotel would have been via the golf course route.

Looking back, I wonder how many of the people in the imaginary 'bus' I gave directions to lived in the same flats as me. Only the lady at the end had asked me where I was going and told me she lived in the flats opposite, but it was quite likely that they all did. With hindsight I wish I'd have asked.

During the time Bob had been out, the water level had risen much higher. Sarah and one of my next door neighbours went upstairs to her flat and decided to stay there. Bob then returned to Camlough Walk to discover it under about four feet of water. He decided to wade through the water, only to find that the main communal door couldn't be opened. This resulted in him having to break in through a downstairs window, before making it through the flood water, up the stairs and finally, his flat.

This group of people then stayed in their flat for the entire night. Sarah even cooked a meal for them all, before leaving the next morning when the water level had subsided.

Even in my focused and slightly delirious state, I was shocked.

'Why did you stay?' I asked.

'In hindsight, we should have left,' said Sarah, 'but at the time it seemed like a good idea.'

Well, fair enough, but having seen my flat the day after, I was glad I'd made the decisions I had that evening.

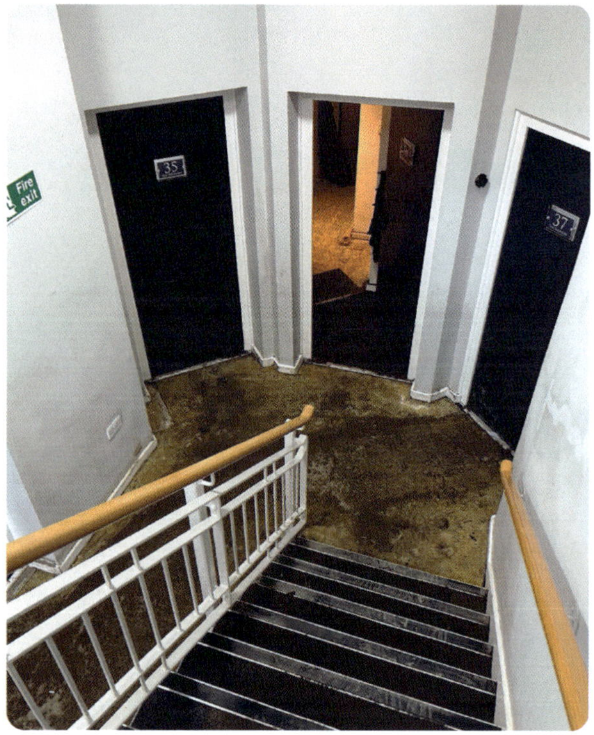

I know some people will wonder, ***'Why did you go to the pub? You could have made it home sooner and maybe saved your stuff!'*** This was certainly something Andrew also thought about. A week later, he mentioned how bad he felt about our pub stop, as if we had kept going, I might have been able to prevent some damage. I told Andrew not to worry; it wouldn't have made any difference.

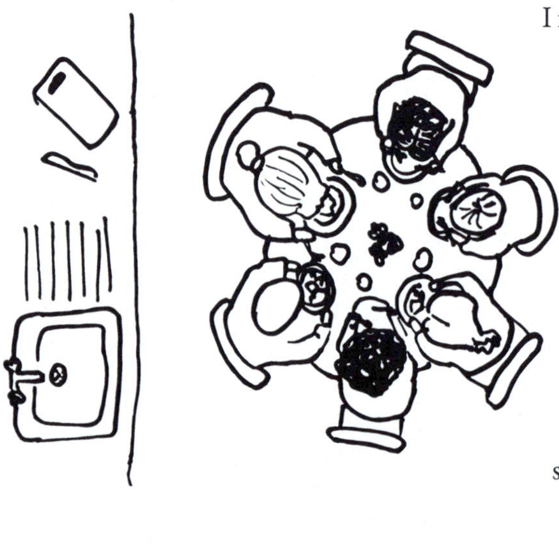

I found out from Sarah that the flat was already flooded by that point. It would be easy to think, I should have set off sooner. But let's be honest, you don't run home every time it starts raining, do you? Even if there is a storm. By the time I was aware the storm was causing a significant amount of damage, it was already too late. In fact, I'm sure that my flat had already flooded when we set off from work.

Bear in mind that this is a ground floor flat, so there is no upstairs to store things safely. Sure, I could have put some items on the worktop, but I'd have still been in the same position of not having anywhere to live.

Back to taking photos and working on my insurance claim. I did this for hours, sifting through all of my personal possessions, to the point I was sick of doing it, but it was worth it. In that one day I took photos of every book I owned, all my clothing, my toiletries and my technology. There was not a single damaged thing I did not photograph. I knew if I did this correctly it would make everything easier in the long run.

I left the flat and drove my car to the car wash as it was entirely covered in flood gunk. I gave it a quick power wash before grabbing my work laptop and heading back to the hotel at around 8.30pm. I always followed the same routine when I entered: I'd drop whatever I was carrying onto the desk, take a quick shower and change into my 'clean' clothes.

I then spent the next few hours at my computer typing up all the items, inserting pictures, and collating all the information as per the insurance company's request. It already ran to forty-three pages and 2,700 words. I know, because I took a photo of it, amazed at how much it had racked up.

It reached the point where I was exhausted and couldn't think anymore, so I decided to go to bed. I would have to sort out some new clothes the following morning. Thankfully, I do have dedicated workwear that is stored at work, so at least I had something new and clean to wear while working.

Going Back to Work

When I arrived at work on Monday morning, Andrew took me aside and told me that I should get on with finding a place to live while I was there.

I'd been so focused on my insurance claim that I had neglected to have a proper look into where to live. Realising that many other people were in the same position, or would be requiring somewhere to rent soon, I decided to spend most of the day contacting estate agents.

When John and Andrew were both at work, we had a chat about the previous Friday and what had happened after we all split up. Normally, I work at my desk in an open plan office but I decided to commandeer a meeting room, not least because it might annoy my colleagues if I was continually on the phone.

The expression 'beggars can't be choosers' comes to mind in respect of the circumstances I found myself in. I knew that the rental market would likely get worse as an influx of flooded residents sought to rent somewhere. I had to be decisive and act fast, so I applied for a few properties that looked decent. I heard back from a few of these and, after explaining my situation, asked for viewings as quickly as possible. A good number had already gone by the time I enquired about them. This seemed to confirm my fears that everyone else was in the same situation and frantically looking for accommodation.

One problem I faced was that the majority of flats had tenants currently living there who would be moving out on a specific date. Naturally, these specific timelines were weeks, or months in some cases, in the future. I didn't have that long to wait; I needed somewhere I could move into immediately.

A couple of the estate agents I contacted moved very quickly, and I soon had two viewings booked in. One of these I was especially excited about. Its only foible, if you could even call it that, was that it was unfurnished. In fact, every flat I came across also seemed to be that way. I thought that looking for a furnished or part-furnished place might make life a little easier; however, at this moment in time, there were seemingly none available. The best news was that the viewing for this flat was the next day. The other one was not until a couple of days' time.

Andrew checked in with me periodically throughout the day, and I told him about the progress I was making, finding suitable accommodation. He was happy to let me go to my viewings during work time, too, in order to find something more quickly.

I also managed to continue building my insurance claim list during this time, mainly when I was tired of looking at rental properties or sending emails and making phone calls. I realised I had missed a couple of items in the photos I was including, so I decided to head to my flat after work to rectify this.

I wasn't there long as I needed to purchase new clothes as a priority. After I had finished, I headed straight to the supermarket across from my hotel. I bought a set of clothes to get me through this until I had time to purchase more. Everything was black, simple and functional.

While putting my new purchases into the hotel wardrobe, I found a dry cleaning order form and bag. Having worn the clothes that Andrew had leant me for the past three days, through flood grunge, sweat and blood, I decided to have them cleaned before giving them back. It felt like the right thing to do. So I bagged them up and filled out the form ready to drop off at reception in the morning. Now to continue with my insurance claim.

In compiling a detailed list of all my damaged belongings, I also had to document the price and a provide a link to where the items could be purchased. I actually had to complete two documents, one for electronic components and one for everything else. This wasn't always straightforward, especially when it came to my book collection. Although, in the main, I didn't own anything that couldn't be replaced, I did lose a couple of signed copies and one rare book. Putting a price on these is difficult, so I did the best I could. After a few more hours I decided it was time to stop for the night.

Tuesday morning began with me dropping off the laundry at reception and grabbing breakfast before heading to work. Even though I had a house viewing in the afternoon, I didn't let up on searching or applying for other properties. Not least to prevent limiting the choice to just one option.

At lunchtime, I set off to view the flat, and was told to meet David, the estate agent, outside. He would be in a red hatchback. Sure enough, I pulled up outside to find him waiting for me. He then showed me around the empty flat. It was fantastic. I'd have to organise furniture but it was at a price I could afford, available immediately and somewhere I could see myself living. I knew that I had to apply.

While talking to David, I explained my situation and asked if I could apply and, if possible, get things moving quickly. He told me I could ring up or, better still, drop by the Chesterfield branch at the Glass Yard off Sheffield Road. With that I headed straight there and David rang them to let them know I was on my way.

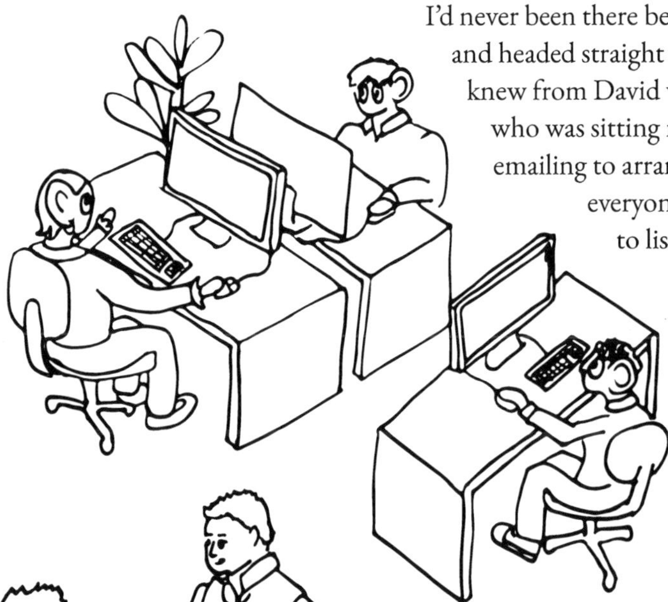

I'd never been there before, but found it without any trouble and headed straight in. I introduced myself to Oscar, who knew from David why I was there. As it transpired, Laura, who was sitting next to Oscar, was the lady I had been emailing to arrange everything. I found it funny that everyone in the office was politely trying not to listen, coupled with the awkward sense of not knowing exactly what they could and couldn't say. I could feel the curiosity in the room so shared some of the story, which you are currently reading, and took out my phone to show them the state of my previous flat. Naturally, this garnered attention from the other estate agents in the room, who formed a small crowd around us as we were discussing things. I think the fact that I was able to laugh and joke about my predicament helped to relieve some of the tension of them being unsure how to react.

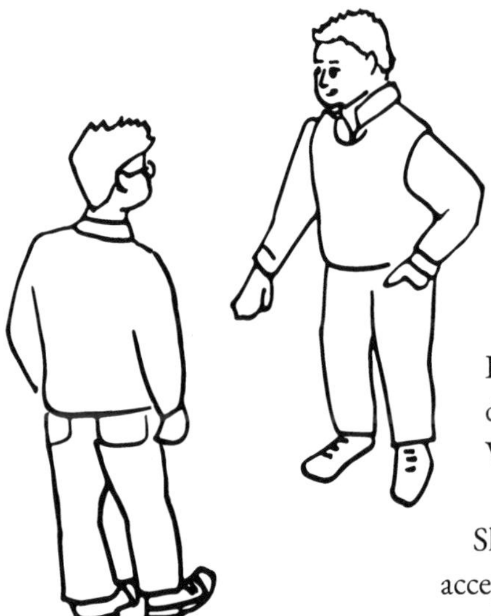

Before I knew it, I had applied for the flat and been informed that, due to the circumstances, I would be fast-tracked through the process. With that I said farewell to my new friends and returned to work.

Shortly after arriving back at work, I received a call saying I had been accepted subject to tenant screening. For those unfamiliar with this process, it basically consists of running a credit check, checking with your employer that you are employed and talking to your references. The only thing that concerned me about this was the time it sometimes took.

Thanks to Lauren, in Human Resources at work, the references and confirmation of my employment were completed rapidly. I remember discussing it with her. 'Don't bother sending anything to Andrew,' she said. 'He'll take too long. Send it to me instead.' Which is why I gave the estate agent Lauren's email address and, to be fair, she was true to her word. I think the form they sent was filled out and sent back within half an hour of her receiving it.

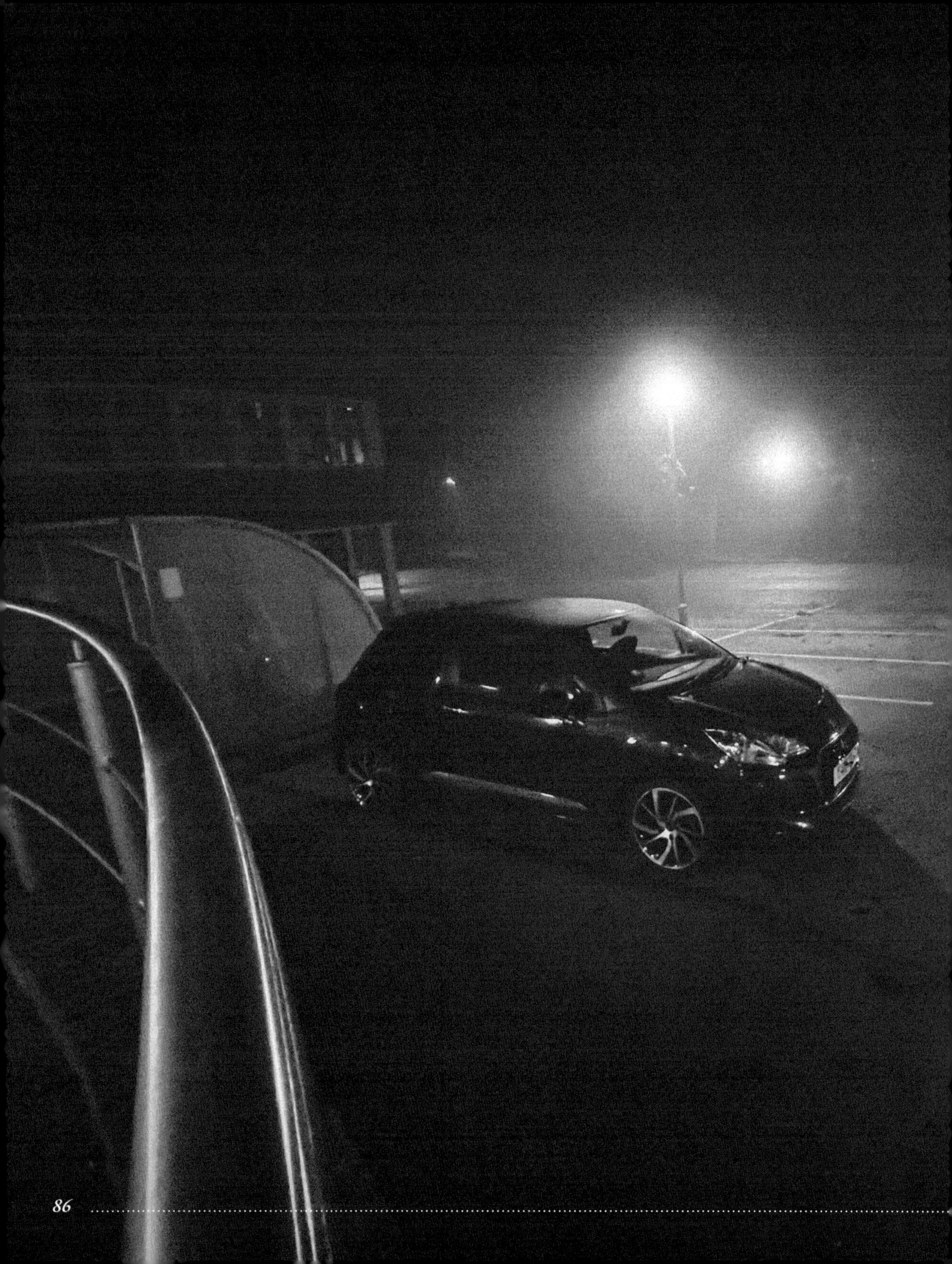

I'd usually stay at work and continue with my insurance claim until late into the night.

I also sent over the holding deposit, which ensured that the flat was taken off the market. This is where money really started to become an issue. I would have to pay out over £1,000 for the deposit plus the first month's rent and then all the associated bills. On top of that, I'd just had to purchase new clothes and restock my toiletries.

Fortunately, while on the phone to my insurance company, I found out they could give me an emergency advance that would be deducted from whatever the total ended up being. This was only £500 but was transferred immediately and really helped with the situation I was in.

At 5pm I had one of my microwave meals at work before heading back to my flat. It was late October and well on its way to being dark. Luckily, the lights had continued to work, so that made it much easier. By now, I was actively clearing out my flat. The council continued to provide several large bins in our street that were collected frequently. I lost count of how many full bin bags I threw in them.

It was a very humbling process. I saw other people experiencing the exact same problems as me, with the street continually full of personal possessions that had been in good and serviceable condition only a few days previously. These would be picked up every day, but the empty space was replaced by a seemingly endless supply of damaged possessions.

I wasn't able to throw everything out straight away, as the insurance company had arranged for a special collection of all my expensive technology items, which included my laptop, camera/lenses and iPad. I was initially concerned about this as some insurance companies send people over to have a look first-hand. I had an image of me throwing everything out and them saying, 'Oh, we need to come and look at everything or you can't claim for it.' As it happens, the company I was with decided this wasn't necessary; however, I still had to document everything.

I assume that most people probably dealt with all this during the day, and I was an oddity for arriving after five to begin the process. I wonder if the upstairs neighbours saw me and thought, ***Who is this crazy man working in the cold and dark?*** I think because of this scheduling I saw less of my neighbours than they did of each other. Then again, I think everyone was too absorbed in their own problems, with their worlds having been turned upside down, to pay much attention to anyone else.

It was now four days after the flood and, by this point, my flat had started to dry out. Don't get me wrong, it still wasn't 'dry', but on the first couple of days there was a top coat of sludge on the floor. Most of this had now hardened to form a solid matt brown surface. This was useful as I had surrendered my previous set of 'dirty' clothes, replacing them with a new set I had bought. Because it was a lot drier I did seem to get less dirty when walking around.

Bizarrely, my old desktop computer survived as it was on a counter that was just a hair higher than the waterline. I eventually stored it in one of the rarely used meeting rooms at the office, along with my three plants and a crate of books that managed to survive. I also put my cleaned toolbox in here too. It was funny seeing these items in a small room as it was the entirety of what survived from my flat. Whenever I made calls to my insurance company during the day, or to estate agents, I would always head into this room; it became my war room.

I'd usually stay at work and continue with my insurance claim until late into the night. Sometimes, I'd take my laptop back to the hotel and do the same, if for no other reason than a change of scenery while completing a boring task. I had hundreds of photos of individual items, such as all my books, electrical items, clothes and kitchen equipment. Some of these images have been included in this book.

Wednesday rolled around with the now familiar routine of heading down for breakfast and then driving to work. This particular morning was slightly different, however, as I had to go to my flat for an hour for a scheduled collection of my electrical items for the insurance company. I had been told to bag each item individually and put them in the special boxes they would provide.

The driver, we'll call him Jim, arrived at the allotted time with two large pink plastic boxes padded with foam. I had never seen them before and asked if anything needed to go in a specific box. I think there was some kind of arbitrary order to which things went where. Jim and I engaged in small talk while this was happening, and he asked why the insurers needed all these items. I explained that it was so they could see if anything could be repaired. I held up my old laptop, which was visibly leaking water, and said:

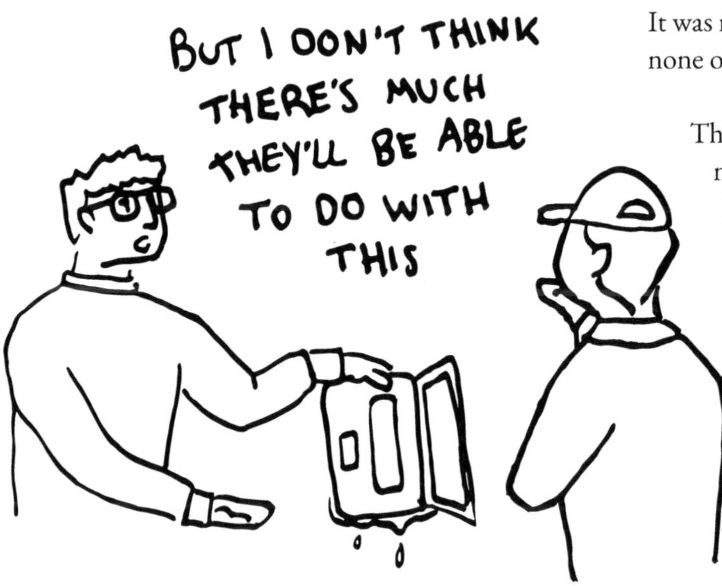

It was rather comical as it was clearly evident that none of it would be repairable.

This was one of two collections they would make. Some of my camera equipment looked less obviously damaged and was going to be sent in separate boxes a week after the first pick-up, this time from my office. As it turned out, none of the electronic items I sent to the insurance company were considered repairable and all were completely dead. Surprise! Surprise! That's what you get for spending twenty-four hours under four feet of dirty flood water!

Just after 10am, I returned to work and immediately checked on the housing situation. The estate agents had worked quickly, and I discovered that my reference checks had all passed. They sent over the contract for me to sign and return digitally, which the landlords also had to do. Again, this was done at a rapid pace, and they signed the same day.

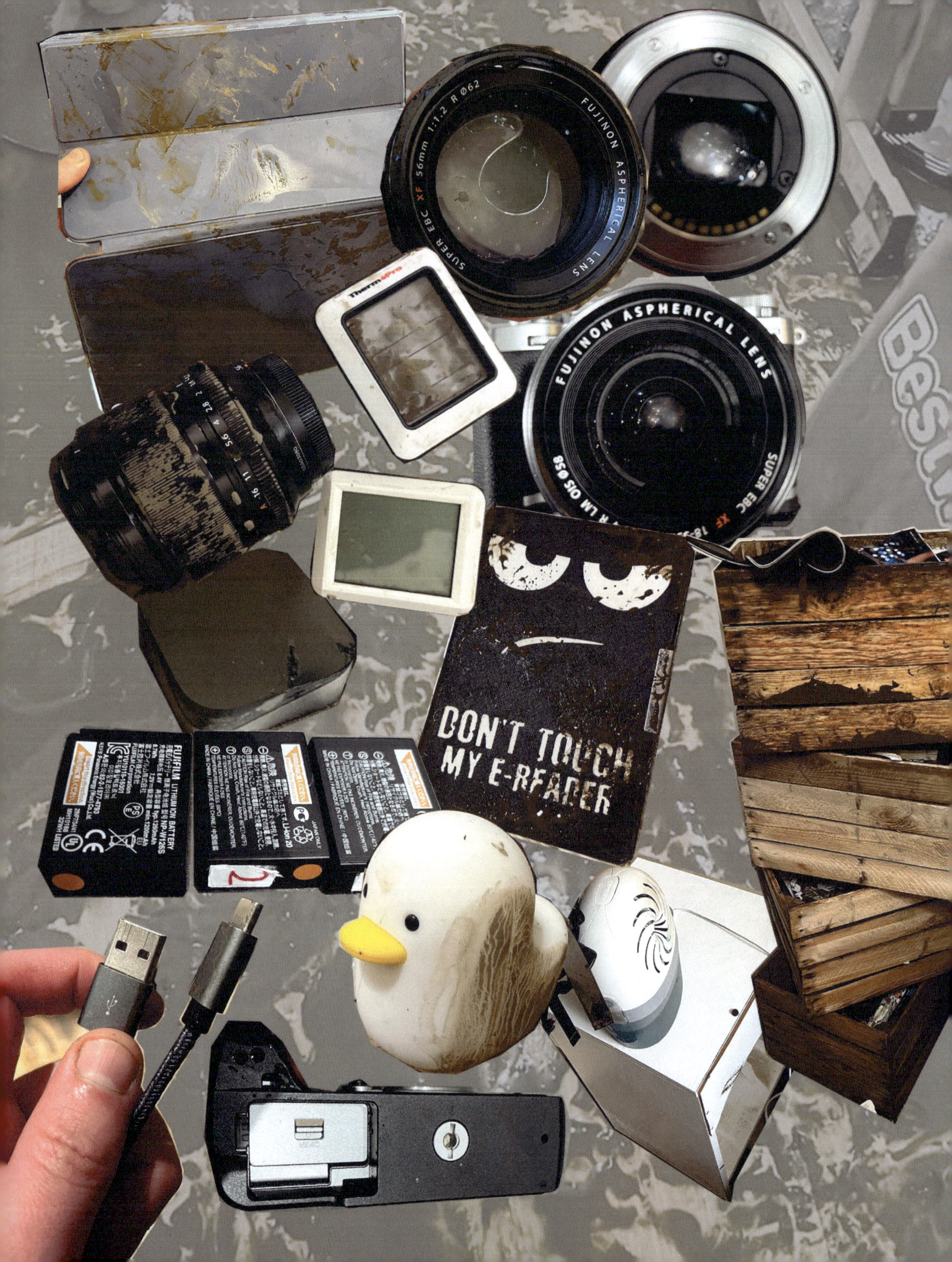

SUPER EBC XF 56mm 1:1.2 R Ø62
FUJINON ASPHERICAL LENS
FUJINON ASPHERICAL LENS
DON'T TOUCH
MY E-READER
FUJIFILM LITHIUM ION BATTERY

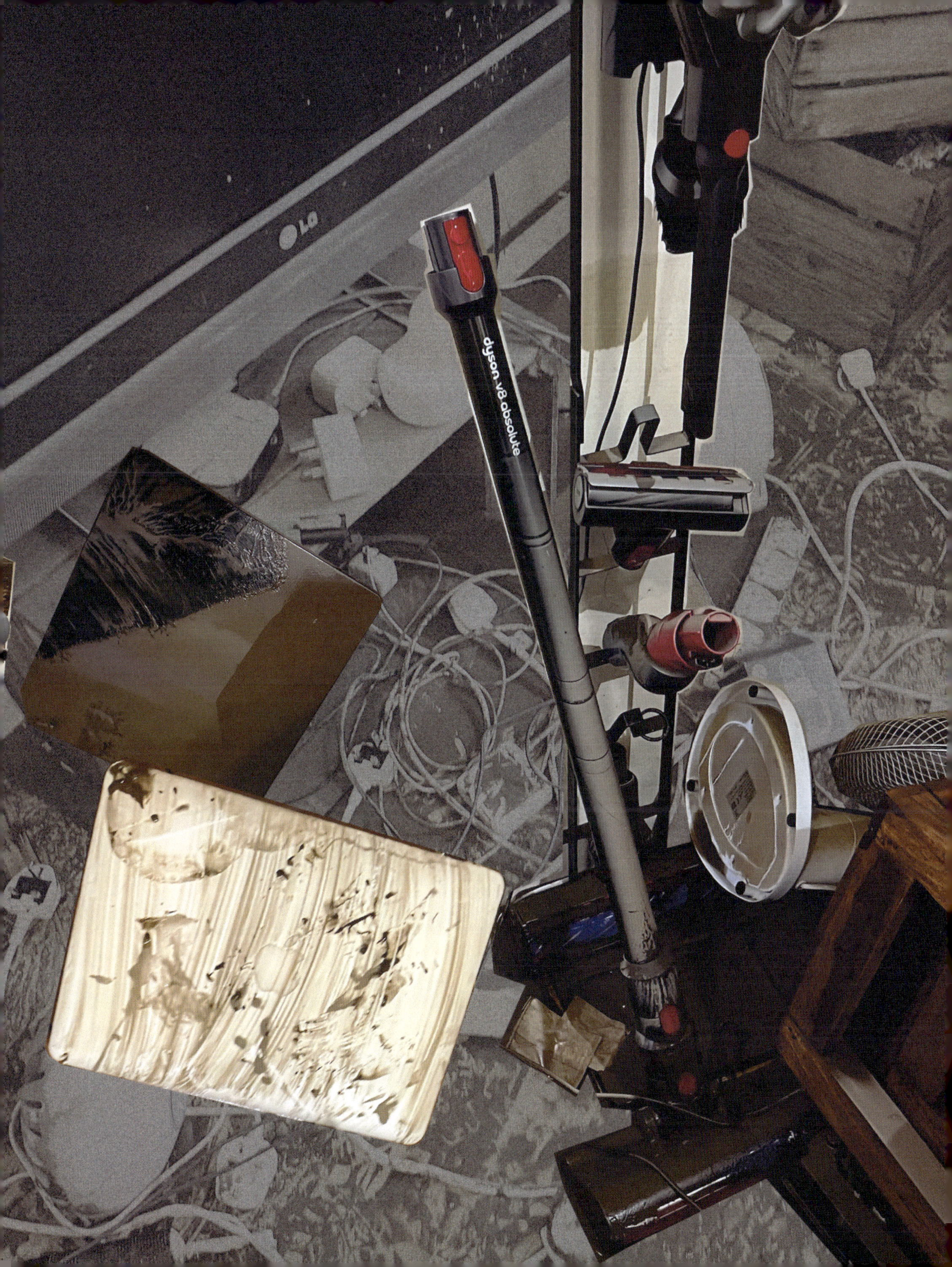
LG
dyson v8 absolute

All in all, it was a good day. I finally felt like I had somewhere to live, and I had made significant progress with my insurance claim. I returned to my hotel to find the clean laundry in my room. Once again, I spent the evening working on the details and costings for my claim.

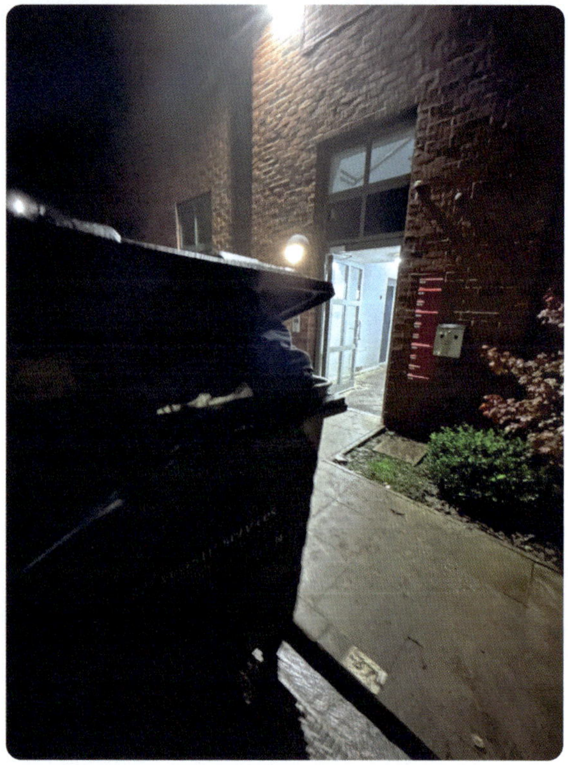

You may be wondering why someone didn't come to the flat to put together the inventory for me. After initially discussing the claim, the insurance advisor suggested that I do the inventory myself. This was so they didn't have to send loss adjusters as their fees would eat into my claimable sum. To be honest, they were right.

As you will realise by now, this was a laborious task that I am certain some people would find difficult, particularly at such at distressing time. I can't imagine what it would have been like to look after children while doing this, or if my grandparents had to face the same situation.

It was now Thursday. My morning routine had begun to feel somewhat normal. Upon entering work I gave Andrew his freshly laundered clothes, for which he was appreciative but said I didn't have to. I'm glad I could repay his kindness even if it was only a small gesture.

I checked my online portal for the rental and discovered that all the required documents had been approved and were ready to go. The last thing I had to do was pay my first month's rent. Again, this put a financial strain on me, but there was nothing I could do. I was stressed about it but knew I could just about get by. I think the comfort of knowing I had somewhere to live, didn't have to worry about my old flat and was going to be reimbursed for my lost items was enough to get me through. It's often easier to concentrate on the negatives, but I realised that I had stormed through the bulk of things I needed to organise. The estate agent arranged a time on Friday when I could pick up the keys. Now it felt much more real.

I lost track of how many hours I spent collating the information for my insurance claim. I'd estimate at least twelve. It was finally at a point I thought it was fully done, though. When I shared these documents with my insurance company they initially assumed they had been uploaded by one of their professional loss adjusters. Upon finding out it was my own work, I was jokingly offered a job there! The insurance assistant told me it was better than some of the professional assessments they were given.

I spent a long time at my flat that day, not leaving until gone 10pm. As the claim was now complete, I was finally able to throw away all of my ruined possessions. This was the day I really felt like I had lost things. Hauling all my books, clothes and personal possessions into a bin felt so wrong. Yet there was nothing I could do about it. My flat felt incredibly empty afterwards. The entire experience made me realise how much stuff we actually have, especially in the UK. We often take how lucky we are for granted.

You might be reading this and wonder how it felt to lose just about everything. It did not bother me losing books, a laptop, a tablet and my camera. Fortunately, my entire digital photo library was backed up in the cloud, as were my important personal files. What really upset me was the irreplaceable items that I can never get back.

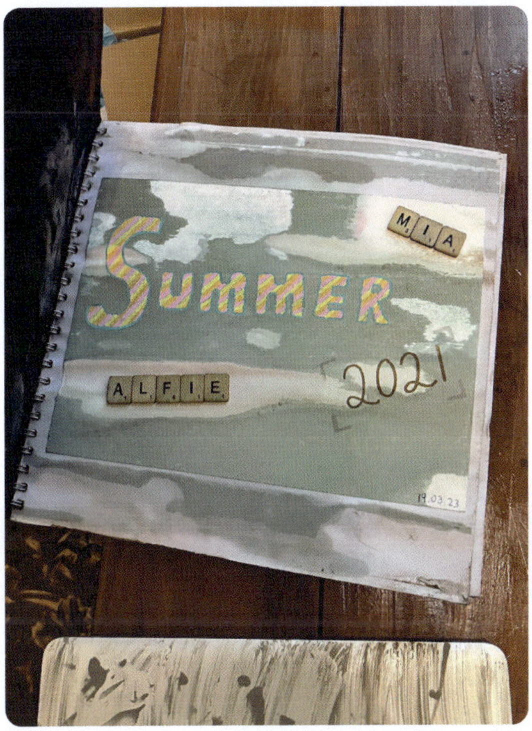

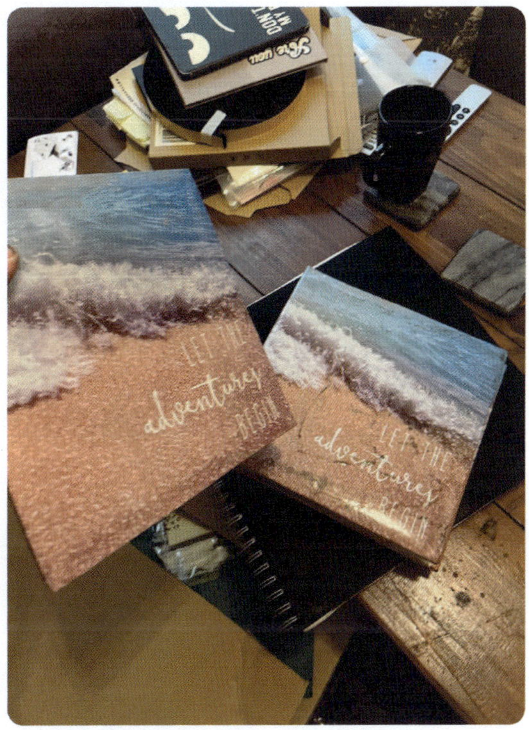

As I mentioned earlier, I owned a couple of signed books that I will be unable to replace. I also had a rare hardback version of a book from 1930 celebrating my company's 100 years in business that will be almost impossible to replace. The loss of these items wasn't so bad. The worst thing that I lost that day was a scrapbook my niece, Mia, and I had made together that detailed a couple of adventures we had been on as a family. As well as featuring digital photos, which can be replaced easily, it also contained her drawings. She was only nine and had spent a year working on it with me at various points doing different drawings for the pages. I will never get these back, and I was truly devastated at their loss.

Most other things were inconvenient, but that hurt.

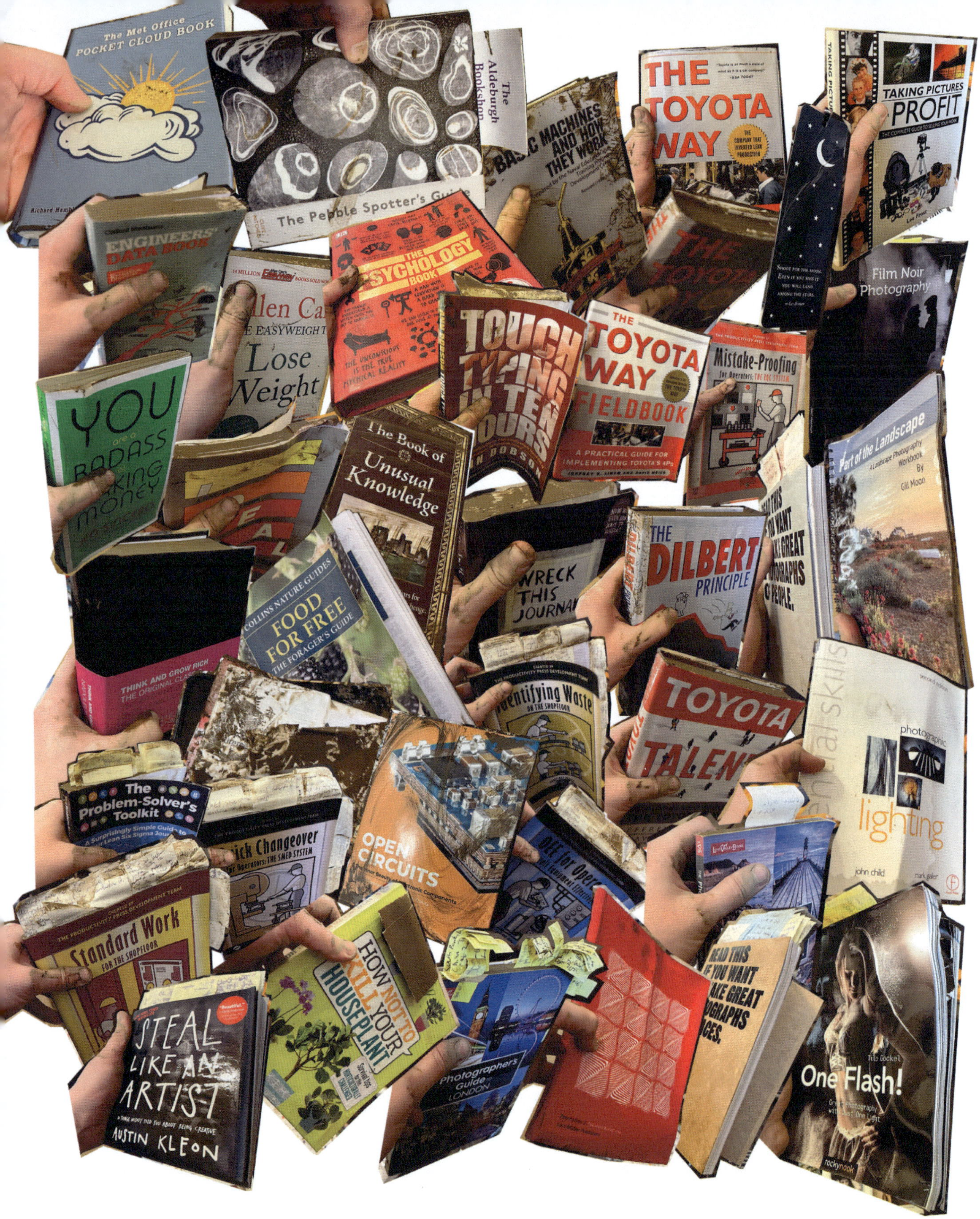
The Met Office POCKET CLOUD BOOK
The Pebble Spotter's Guide
The Aldeburgh Bookshop
BASIC MACHINES AND HOW THEY WORK
THE TOYOTA WAY
TAKING PICTURES FOR PROFIT
ENGINEERS' DATA BOOK
Lose Weight
THE PSYCHOLOGY BOOK
TOUCH TYPING IN TEN HOURS
THE TOYOTA WAY FIELDBOOK
A PRACTICAL GUIDE FOR IMPLEMENTING TOYOTA'S 4Ps
Mistake-Proofing
Film Noir Photography
YOU are a BADASS
The Book of Unusual Knowledge
Part of the Landscape
A Landscape Photography Workbook
By Gill Moon
WRECK THIS JOURNAL
THE DILBERT PRINCIPLE
COLLINS NATURE GUIDES
FOOD FOR FREE
THE FORAGER'S GUIDE
THINK AND GROW RICH
TOYOTA TALENT
photographic lighting
john child
The Problem-Solver's Toolkit
Quick Changeover
OPEN CIRCUITS
Standard Work
FOR THE SHOPFLOOR
HOW NOT TO KILL YOUR HOUSEPLANT
STEAL LIKE AN ARTIST
AUSTIN KLEON
Photographer's Guide to LONDON
One Flash!
rockynook

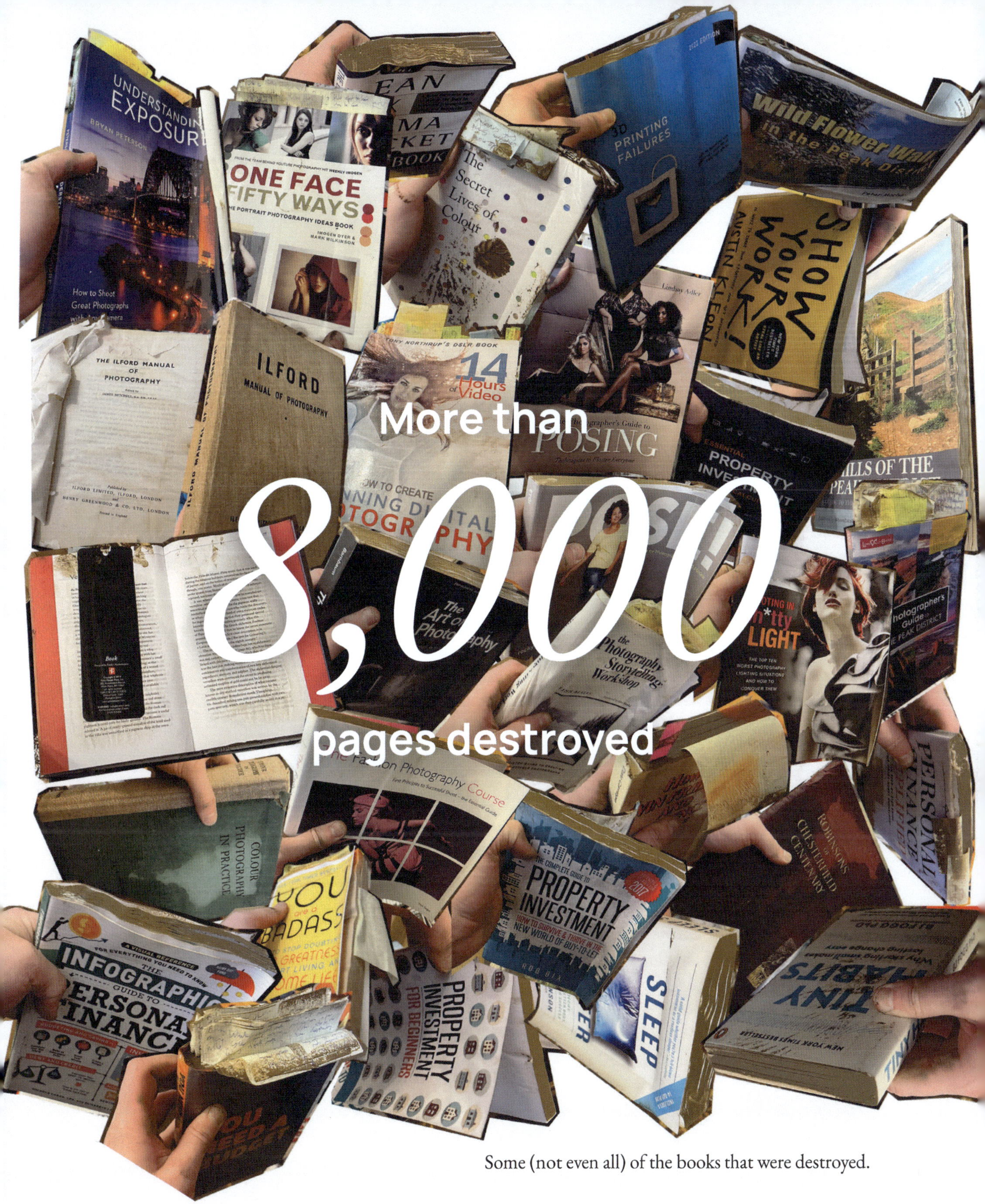

Some (not even all) of the books that were destroyed.

Handing Back the Keys

During this week, I was in frequent contact with my old landlord, who was under pressure from the building's owners to have everyone's possessions out in under a week to allow them to rip up the flooring and let the building dry out. While he was very understanding and told me to take my time, I didn't want to take any longer than was necessary. Dragging this out was pointless, and I needed to act swiftly so that I could move on with my life.

While I kept in high spirits and did my best to remain positive, my body somewhat betrayed the stress I was under. This culminated in nose bleeds that would occur randomly. I didn't actively discuss this with anyone, and did my best to be discreet about it, as I could just sneak away and deal with it in private. However, it did occur at inconvenient moments. Imagine standing in an open plan office having a chat with the plant manager, production manager, engineering manager, process engineer and quality manager. (Yes, I did manage to do some work during this week.) Then, mid-conversation my nose started to bleed. There was a worried look on people's faces as I tapped under my nose with my hand to check it was blood before calmly making my excuses. I think my colleagues were concerned, but it was something I got used to and was able to deal with. So I apologised and walked to the kitchen alongside a concerned Andrew.

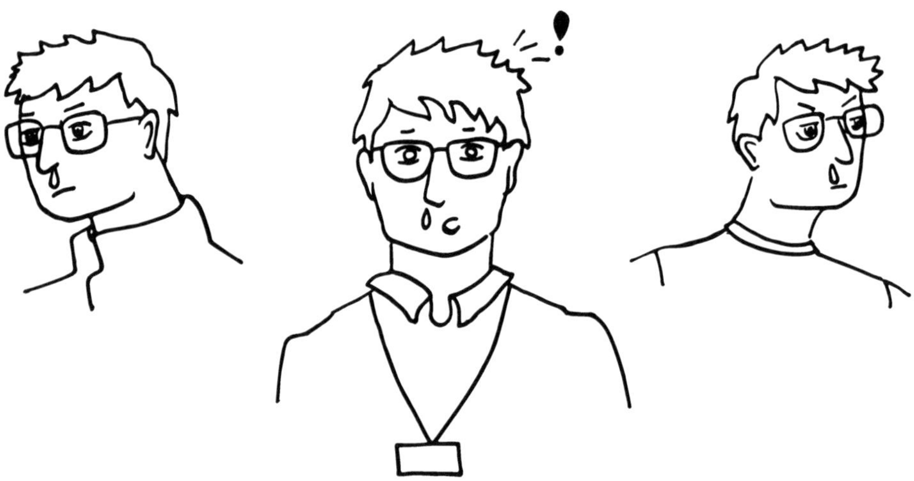

This happened sporadically throughout my adventures that week, usually at the worst possible times. At work or in a supermarket. One of my favourites was in the hotel lift on the way to my room. I worried that there'd be a group of people waiting at the doors, staring at me with blood all over my face and hands as I held my nostrils together. Couple that with wearing dirty flood clothes and I looked somewhat dishevelled! This thought occurred to me while I was alone in the lift, which made me laugh out loud. Great! Now I look even more crazy. Luckily, there wasn't anyone there when the doors opened.

On Thursday evening I went back to my flat and continued to remove my belongings; however, there were no more photos to take or documentation to complete. For once, I didn't have to spend the entire evening on a laptop putting a claim together. I spent longer at my flat that night. Without any means of heating, it was always freezing, but this was the first time I'd really taken notice of it. When you're running around carrying things back and forth you soon build up some warmth.

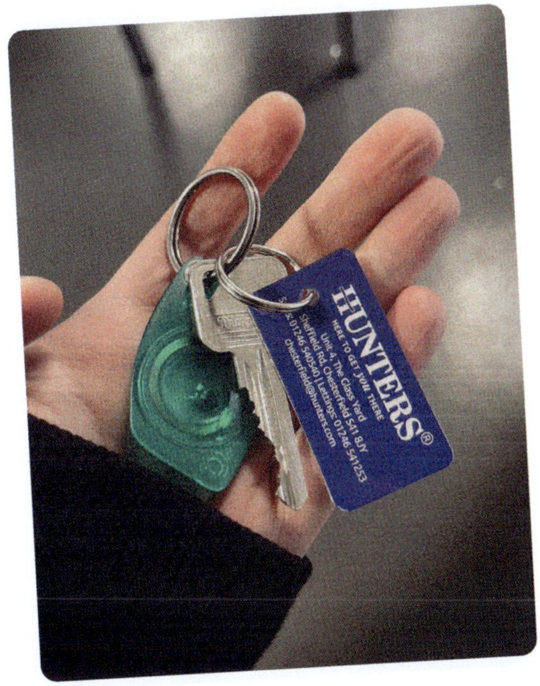

Friday morning came around and I went to work. It was a lovely morning and day; the sun was bright and the air was crisp and pleasant. At lunchtime I picked up the keys for my new flat from the estate agent and headed straight over to have another look. I didn't need to, because it wasn't going anywhere, but it felt like celebrating a victory.

Back at work, I talked to Andrew and John about what we had been up to at that time the week before. I remember us trying to work out if we were in the pub drinking 'Drowned Rat' or not.

The sun hung low in the sky that evening as everyone left the factory for the weekend. I filled my car with the few belongings that had survived and had been stored in my 'war room'. I then drove to my new flat and dumped everything on the empty floor of my new living room.

I then discovered a rather large inconvenience I hadn't thought about. I had not transferred the internet from my old flat to this new one. As it was a somewhat rural location, there was no phone signal either. This was a big problem as I needed to set up council tax, electric, gas and all the other associated paraphernalia you go through with moving.

I also realised I'd need some essentials for this new flat, like toilet roll, towels, hand wash and cleaning materials. The more I considered it, the longer the list became. It was funny, I thought I had 'finished', yet in reality, I was just beginning. I then spent the evening ensuring I had what I needed for the new flat. This was a nice change of pace, to be honest.

Earlier in this book I mentioned having lived in various rentals as a student and working in different locations around the country. Naturally, this means I have dealt with a fair few estate agents. Well, I have to say that this was probably the best experience I'd ever had. I certainly appreciate the effort that the estate agent and new landlord put into expediting the process.

Saturday morning came around and I changed into my 'dirty' set of clothes, once again, before heading over to my old flat. There were only a couple of things I needed to move to my new home now, the main thing being a set of step ladders. I made sure these were fully clean before dropping them off at my new flat.

I then confirmed that I had thrown everything away, ensuring that not a single possession was left behind. It was odd seeing the flat empty like that. It was completely devoid of any of my personality now, just like it had been when I initially moved in.

One of the last things I did was to leave my keys in a bowl on the kitchen worktop, letting the landlord know that I had finished moving out. I even took a photo as the final goodbye to my old flat. That was the last time I set foot in that building. Well, sort of!

I called it a night and returned to the hotel, much earlier than I had done previously. I decided to eat in the restaurant and enjoyed a beer and a roast duck breast as a celebration. It was utterly fantastic. I turned on the TV for the first time during my stay and watched something while comparing internet, gas and electric deals on my phone.

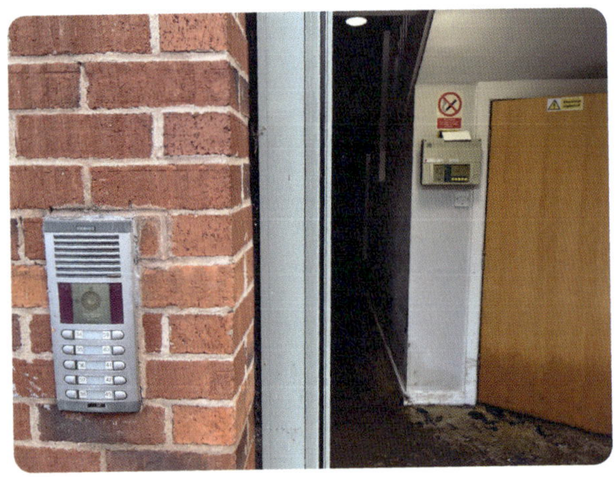

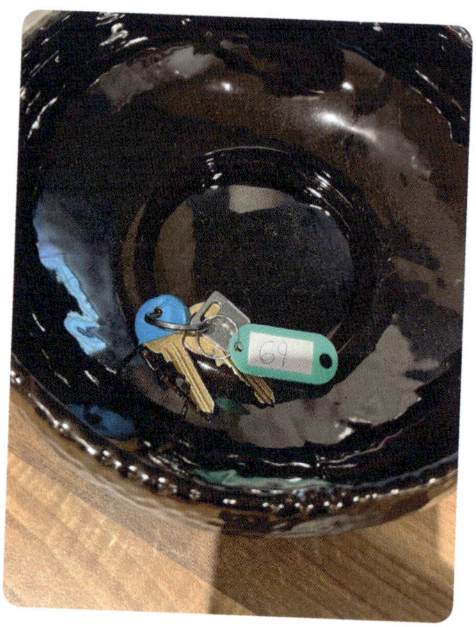

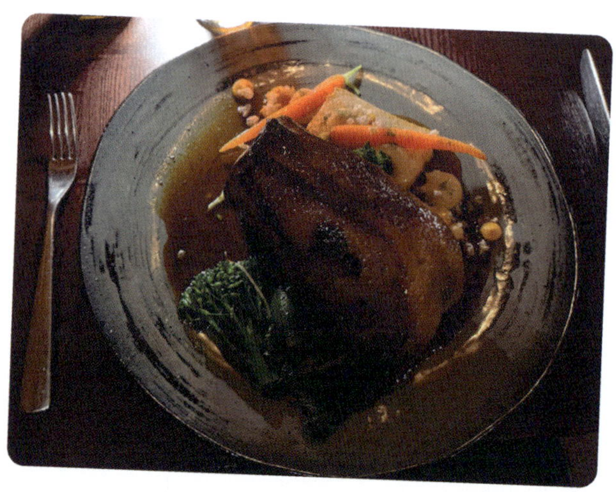

Leaving the Hotel

I checked out of the Casa on Sunday morning and headed to a hotel in Swindon to attend a photography workshop I had booked many months prior. I couldn't change this so had to make the best of it. Luckily, I had already booked the week off work, which would prove useful as it allowed me time to sort out my new flat on my return.

By this point, I'd spent just over a week at the Casa Hotel. It was a great source of comfort for me while I was sorting things out. I do not think I could have operated as effectively as I did if I hadn't had such a comfortable place to stay. I think I was spoilt by the experience as when I arrived at the cheap hotel where the workshop was being held, I immediately felt the difference. I was tremendously fortunate that my work supported me during this difficult time.

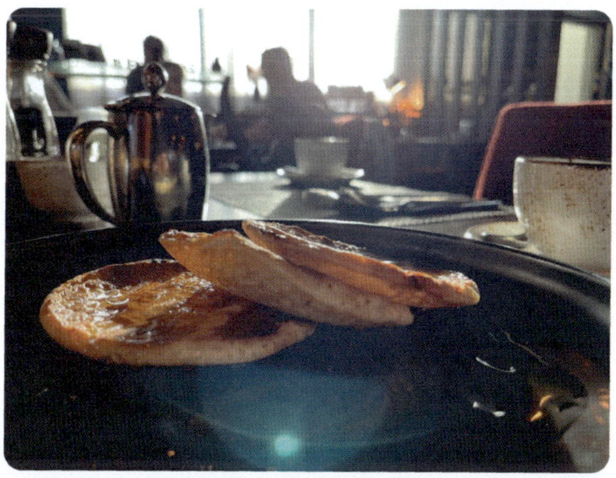

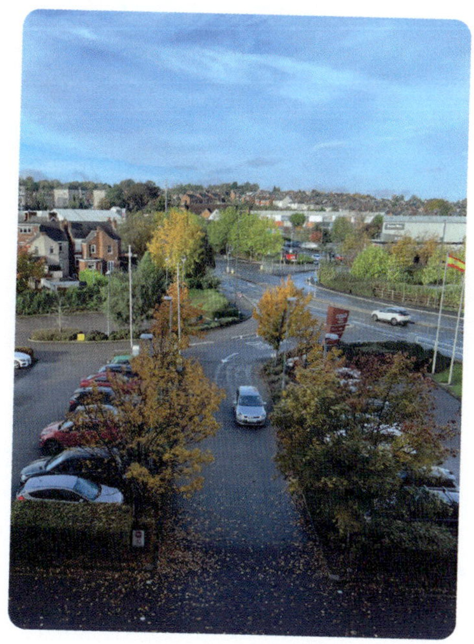

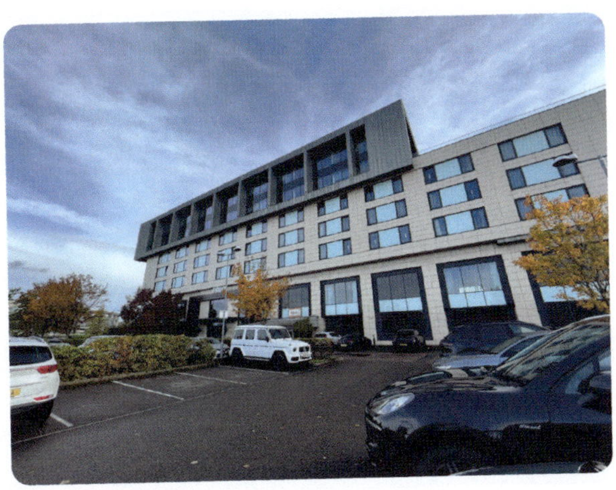

A great deal had happened in a week. My home had been flooded, I'd put together an insurance claim report, thrown away most of my belongings, salvaged what little I could, arranged flat viewings, secured a new flat, managed to scrape together a deposit and moved what little I had left into my new home.

Distancing myself from it all for a while was nice. I didn't have to stare at everything I had to deal with constantly and could have a real break. I hadn't really stopped since this all began.

It was an exhausting week to say the least, but not the end of this journey.

I had a week off work, but naturally it wasn't going to be as relaxing as I had hoped. After a single night in Swindon I went back to Hull, where I spent a couple of days sourcing the furniture and appliances that I needed. I already owned a bed and enlisted the help of my dad to drive a van to bring it to Chesterfield. We also picked up a washing machine on the way.

We drove to Chesterfield and built my bed in my new bedroom before installing the washing machine. We then went to pick up a fridge-freezer which had been kindly donated by my work colleague, Kevin. This was a busy day. My dad took the van back the same day, and I stayed in my new flat for the first time.

One question that continually cropped up was whether I had moved into a flat that wasn't on the ground floor. My response was always the same. 'No, my new flat is on the ground floor.' I would follow this up by asking them if their house had a ground floor. I always found the 'oh yeah' that followed to be amusing before telling them not to worry as the location was a significantly higher elevation so wasn't likely to flood.

I spent the next few days arranging the necessary services for my new flat. Annoyingly, it would take a couple of weeks for the internet to go live. This meant every time I needed to make a phone call I had to do it at work or drive into town. This is not the most convenient arrangement when you have a lot to organise. As a result, I went into work some evenings to do this.

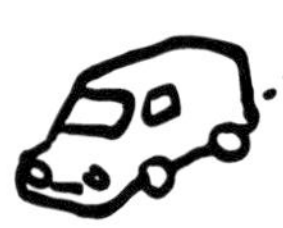

The Follow-Up

It only took a few weeks for the insurance company to pay out the full amount of my claim for my contents. During this time, the only real furniture I had in my flat was a bed and a camping chair.

The insurance advisors I spoke to said that my claim had gone through so quickly because of the detailed paperwork I had provided. Unfortunately, the sum I received didn't quite cover everything; however, it was the maximum I was insured for. It is hard to know the maximum amount you should insure your contents for when taking out these policies, and you often underestimate how much you actually have. I suppose most people, myself included, don't expect to have to claim for all of their belongings in one go.

If you are a homeowner reading this, firstly get contents insurance if you don't already have it, and secondly, really think about how much everything you own costs and make sure you leave some headroom for anything you may purchase in the future. All the things you don't think of can quickly add up, such as electric toothbrushes, aftershave, perfume, electric razors, vacuum cleaners and clothing. Following this experience, I increased the value of my contents insurance.

With that said, I can't fault my insurance company. They were very attentive, took calls reasonably quickly and were efficient in organising prompt collection of damaged items. They kept me up to date at all times and sent me an emergency payment to help with expenses.

Without doubt, it would have been easier to have a loss adjuster come and document everything. However, I would have been charged a lot for the privilege. This charge would be taken from the maximum amount I could claim for. After hearing about the situation and looking at photos I had sent in, the insurance advisor suggested that I do the documentation myself as, from experience, they thought I would be hitting the maximum of my policy. Although I had a lot of extra work to do, this turned out to be fantastic advice. I cannot fault how I was treated and how quick they were to process the full payment of my claim.

It took about five months for me to buy furniture and replace most of my damaged items. Naturally, this was an incredibly expensive time, and I was constantly getting deliveries and shopping for this or that. I remember spending these months on a camping chair with no other furniture in my living room apart from the handful of items that had survived. I was also very fortunate that my grandad helped to support me during this time, and he paid for a new sofa suite.

It was January 2024 when my sofas arrived, and by February my living room had been transformed into an actual living space. I'm currently writing this sitting on one of those sofas, with a coffee in hand, thinking back to how I didn't have a kettle or toaster for a month and used to boil water in a pan to make a coffee.

Something I learnt during this time was just how comfortable we actually have it in this day and age. Compared with all of past humanity, we live in what could be considered luxury. It took having this taken away and then slowly regaining it to realise just how lucky I am. Next time you step into a shower and feel the warm water on your head, take a moment to pause and think about how only fifty or sixty years ago, the majority of people would not have had this privilege. Now practically everyone in the UK has access to a shower, but how many times do you stop to appreciate it?

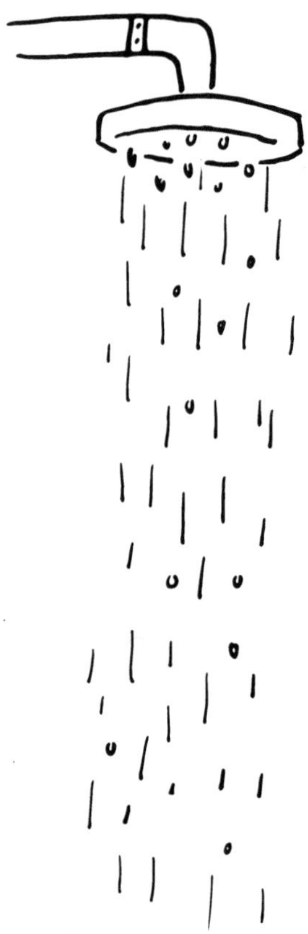

Council Tax Shennanigans

Just before I moved out of my flooded flat, flat, Chesterfield Council rang me and said that I qualified for the flood scheme and would receive £500 cash. I was also told that I would be exempt from paying council tax for a minimum of three months. They added that this would be transferred if I changed my local authority. I told them I had already done so and had no intention of moving back. Fantastic, I thought, some useful financial help. It was thanks to this grant that I was able to pay the first month's rent upfront for my new flat when I was really struggling financially.

Unfortunately, I had no end of issues with council tax due to this. I didn't discover this until around April 2024. Chesterfield Council told me I hadn't paid the £283 that was owed for the flooded Camlough Walk flat, even though I directly asked if there was anything I needed to pay when I moved. I was told I had 'fully paid up' and didn't need to do anything else as they would handle it on my behalf. What made this worse was the £35 summons fee. And, yes, I received a summons for this unpaid amount, because I didn't know anything about it until this point.

When I queried this I was told that the recordings on the phone are deleted after three months, so there was no proof, and that they had tried to contact me via email. Naturally, there was no way of me proving I hadn't received anything, so I had to pay it.

As if this wasn't enough, I rang my new council (North East Derbyshire) and asked why my direct debit payments weren't coming out as the time had elapsed for my flood scheme. They then informed me that I didn't have a direct debit, even though I clearly remember setting one up when I opened my account with them.

I asked the council to set this up and take what was due, to which I was told they couldn't as I was on the flood scheme exemption list. I told them that mine should have run out by now, but they told me that it wasn't how it worked and that I wasn't entitled to it in the first place, even though they had previously requested proof from Chesterfield Council, and I would have to pay the full amount. I explained the situation and they said that they would need to undertake a review and that this would take a month.

Naturally, in both cases I raised complaints, and it took until mid-June for them to get back to me. It made no difference; they charged me for all of it. At a time when I was depending on the information from the council to be accurate and correct, I was let down. I would have preferred it if they hadn't mentioned anything about council tax; then there would have been no problem.

What I find incredibly frustrating is that I have never missed a tax payment other than the present time when, due to extenuating circumstances and being directly told I didn't owe anything, I was penalised for it. I think what's worse is that neither council seemed to care. There was no empathy or understanding, just a cold response. They wouldn't consider any option other than I was at fault. I only hope that the families and vulnerable people affected by this flood were treated better than I was in the aftermath.

To add some degree of balance to this, as previously mentioned, Chesterfield Council did well in the clean-up after the event and provided efficient refuse collection for flooded possessions. The grant that I received from them was also invaluable. At the very least, I thank them for that.

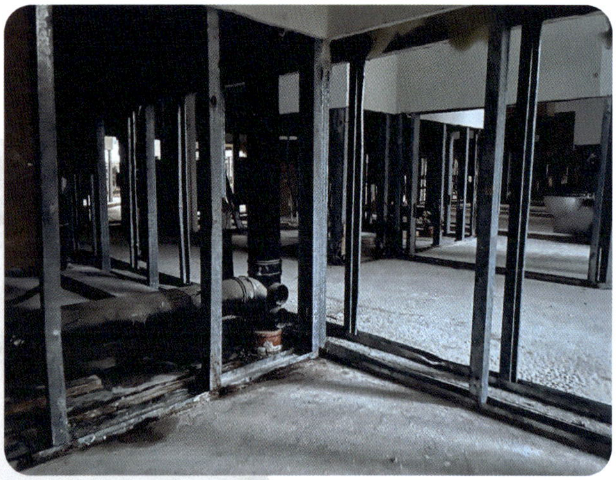

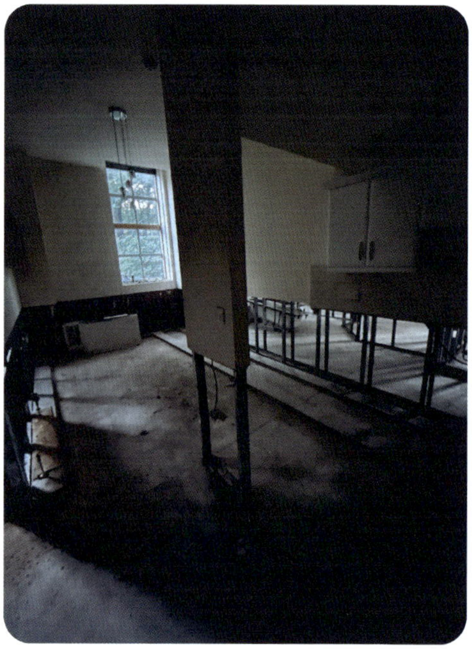

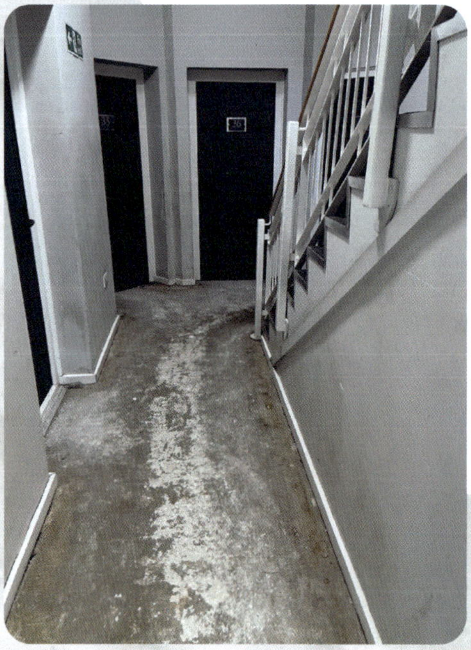

A Year On: The Foundry Building

In late June of 2024, I reached out to my old landlord to see how he was getting on after the flood. I was expecting to hear a story of how it had been a nightmare for a few months, while the building work took place, but that things had now settled down and a new tenant had moved in.

This is not what happened.

'You want to see the flat as of last Sunday?' my landlord's message read.

'Yeah, sure,' I replied.

Eight months after the flood I was sent a photo of my old flat. It had been completely stripped. The bottom half of the walls were gone, the bathroom completely ripped out as well as the kitchen.

It turns out that there was an issue between the leaseholders, building owners and their insurance company. As a result, the bottom of the building had been ripped out; however, no work had been done to refurbish it. According to my landlord, the case had gone to court, resulting in months of online negotiations and legal action.

Curiosity compelled me to take a look for myself. I walked through the communal hallway unable to believe that it looked much the same as it had the last time I was there. I entered my old flat.

By this point in time everything in the wider environment seemed to be back to normal. And yet, here I was facing the aftermath again.

I took some photos of the inside of my flat to share with you. Gutted of its interior with only the shell left behind. The bottom few feet of wall were completely missing. This meant you could easily see across the long building into all the other ground floor flats. All of which were in the same state as mine. It wasn't a flat anymore; sadly it wasn't a building site either. It felt more like an abandoned building. An eerie silence haunted the air.

Over a year after the flood in November 2024 flat 37 appeared on the property market – the interior stripped bare, with the bottom half of the walls still missing. Browsing through the photos I could see into my flat, which looked the same. It was up for auction. I suspect that a year of headaches and stress had led the owner to try to move on. And who can blame them? I wonder if my old flat will meet the same fate. And how long it will be until it's habitable. Maybe it never will be.

Most of Chesterfield had seemingly recovered. There were no obvious scars to see on the surface. Which made me wonder how many other people were still dealing with the consequences of that day. Hidden in the backstreets and behind building facades. Yet, behind closed doors, this was the reality.

I was incredibly lucky with my experience of the flood. Only losing material items.

That wasn't the case for some people who lost friends and loved ones.

I decided to write this book to share my experience of the 2023 Chesterfield flooding. This was a significant event that those affected can now share with those who didn't experience it first-hand in the hope it will lead to action being taken to prevent future flooding. This could be in the form of climate change reform or improvements to civil engineering and infrastructure.

I hope that councils investigate and implement stronger flood defence measures. I know that Hull has spent a great deal on flood prevention schemes since the 2007 floods. I hope Chesterfield Council and the surrounding areas also decide to invest in measures that will safeguard against this occurring again. I understand they have invested in this already to some degree, which is great, but I'm sure we'd all like to see further improvements.

To be completely honest, this book also serves another purpose: To remind you that even when hardships arise you can get through them. Things can always be much worse, so count your blessings for today.

Thank you for accompanying me on this commute through Storm Babet. I hope your mushy peas stay frozen and you don't attempt to swim across flooded roads.

I consider myself to be a fiercely independent person. It's how I have always been, even as a child. With that said, it would not have been possible to get through this experience as smoothly as I did without the help and support of a few key people.

With that in mind, I would like to show my gratitude for specific acts of kindness I experienced during a rough time.

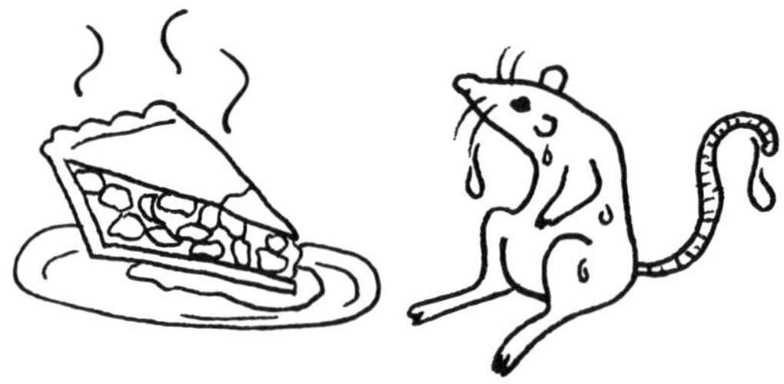

To John and Andrew, thank you for being companions on our adventure to commute across Chesterfield. I asked both of them for their permission to include our story and photos in a publicly available book, to which they agreed.

To Andrew, thank you for hosting me for the evening and allowing me time to sort things out during my working hours. Plus, letting me drink all your beer!

And thanks to my company for covering the cost of the hotel bill. I achieved more in a week then I could have in a month without that help.

Lauren, our work's Human Resources manager, thank you for dealing with all the associated paperwork and references in such a quick manner as to allow me to move in within a week.

To Christina, thank you for letting me eat your steak pie. And for laundering my clothes.

To my Dad, thank you for helping me to move furniture and for driving a hired van to shift fridges, beds and washing machines.

To my grandad and nana, thank you for supporting me over the phone and helping me to purchase furniture.

To Kevin, thank you for gifting me a fridge.

And Ann for giving me an iron.

To all my friends and work colleagues, thank you for being understanding and kind while this was all going on.

To the staff at the Casa Hotel who made my stay so pleasant, thank you all.

To my estate agents, Hunters, thank you everyone for being so caring and pushing things through quickly so that I wasn't homeless for long. Laura, Oscar and David, you worked hard on everything, and I really appreciate it.

To all of you who also experienced the flood first-hand, I hope your stories have got a little brighter as time has gone on and we have rebuilt.

And, finally, to you, the reader, thank you for purchasing my book and taking the time to read my story.

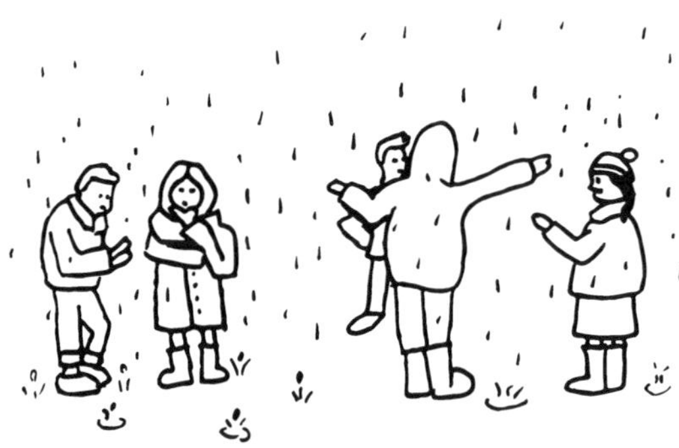

Printed in Great Britain
by Amazon

57614085R00064